BEYOND THE HOUSE
OF SILENCE

Secrets Layered upon Secrets

Beyond the House of Silence

of Silence

Secrets Layered upon Secrets

**Arlene R. Taylor PhD
Marilyn J. Banford PhD**

Success Resources International
Napa, California

Dedication

This book is dedicated to survivors everywhere and to the therapists and specialists who believed in them and who helped them find their voices.

Acknowledgements

This book would never have been written without the support of many people, some of whom didn't even realize the extent of their contribution. I am forever grateful.

Some of you know who you are.

Thank you.

Publisher's Reminder

This book is not a biological, medical, or psychological text. The information and resources offered are for general educational and informational purposes only and do not present an in-depth treatment of specific research findings or topics. They are not intended to take the place of professional counseling, medical or psychological care, recovery therapy, or recommendations from healthcare professionals.

Be sure to consult with your physician, therapist, or healthcare professional before you make lifestyle changes or implement recovery strategies.

The publisher, author, contributors, and editors expressly disclaim all responsibility and any liability (direct or indirect) for adverse effects from the use or misuse of concepts presented herein.

If you find errors / typos in this book, please know that they are there for a purpose. Some brains really enjoy looking for mistakes…

Table of Contents

Chapter Notes   **Page**

There Is No Agony Like
An Untold Story
Inside Of You.

—Maya Angelou

Intro—
In the Beginning

The conflict between the will to deny horrible events and the will to proclaim them aloud is the central dialectic of psychological trauma.

—Judith Lewis Herman

"Can we talk?" The woman was tall and trim. "You understand this is very uncharacteristic for me. I've never asked to talk with a speaker before." Her thick dark hair was cut in a wedge, a style I would have loved to wear had my head been blessed with that abundance of hair.

Tired, after almost a full day of speaking, I might have excused myself, but a curiosity niggled at the back of my mind. There was something familiar about her, so I answered, "Sure. Let's meet in the lounge after tonight's presentation." The woman nodded and moved away, walking with an athletic stride. But her shoulders were stooped, and there was an almost furtive look about her. Ah, she was the *jumpy* woman I had noticed the night before.

1

Friday evening while standing at the back of the auditorium waiting for my first presentation to begin, I had watched attendees stream in, greet friends, and find seats. This same woman had entered, moved a chair to the side, and sat down with her back to the wall. Even more eye-catching was her state of high alertness.

At the tiniest sound—the scraping of a chair, the closing of a door, a whispered comment, the clasp clicking on a pocketbook, a cough or sneeze, a book falling to the floor—the woman would tense and glance around apprehensively. Something was making her very, very jumpy. Walking to the stage a few minutes later, however, I tucked away those observations to focus on my presentation.

As guest speaker, my topic for the weekend was how PET Scans (Positron Emission Tomography) were beginning to revolutionize what was known about the brain. As other brain-imaging equipment emerged, the collective body of knowledge would come to be known as the science of brain function. Already I was enthralled with some of the study conclusions and loved sharing the information, packaged in a way I hoped would stimulate others to take an interest in the brain and learn more about it.

That Saturday evening, as arranged, I waited in the lounge, wondering if the *jumpy* woman would show. She did. We sat, one at each end of a long dark-green sofa against a wall in the hotel lounge. (Eventually I would learn that she never sat with her back exposed in a room.)

After initial pleasantries that included learning her first name (a pseudonym for purposes of this book), I asked, "So, what's on your mind, Amelia?"

"Nothing," she replied. *Nothing?* It seemed her entire body was vibrating, palpably humming with some strong emotion. I took a guess.

"Are you angry about something?" She stared at me. "Is your brain angry about something?" I repeated, thinking to depersonalize the question by using the word *brain.*

This time she answered, emphatically. "Of course not. Why would my brain be *angry?*"

"I have no idea," I replied.

"What would I have to be angry *about?*"

"I don't know. Anger is the emotion that arises when a person's boundaries have been invaded, providing information and energy to take appropriate action." Amelia squirmed.

Thinking Amelia was about to bolt from the room, I changed the subject. "Do you like sports?" That turned out to be a safe topic. Yes, Amelia loved sports, almost all sports. There were a fist-full of challenging activities with which she was involved, either currently or in the past. She reeled off a list of team competitions, winnings, awards, and recognitions—a fairly staggering list—so extensive I began to wonder what sport existed she had not tried!

As we chatted, her body gradually stopped vibrating. Stopped, that is, until I circled back around and asked about her family

"Tell me about your childhood. Did anything scary happen to you during childhood?" The palpable humming returned with a vengeance.

"Are you kidding?" she exploded. "Why would you ask such a question? That's ridiculous. Of course nothing scary happened to me. I had great parents. I had a wonderful childhood!"

As she spoke, I watched her facial expression change from one of warm sports enthusiasm to an icy closed-down apprehension. A shuttered, almost haunted look crept into her eyes.

This woman is terrified about something, I thought to myself. *Although her brain is refusing to acknowledge it at a conscious level, her body is definitely doing so at a subconscious level.* Again I changed the subject, asking some innocuous question and listening as she chatted about this, that, and the other thing. Safe, superficial. Mostly about her love of sports and nature.

As we prepared to go our separate ways for the night, I threw out a last comment: "There is usually a reason for a brain being angry. You might want to explore that." Amelia said nothing. She just stared at me through those inscrutable eyes. Then turning abruptly, she rapidly scurried away. Almost running.

Reaching my room I was startled to discover that Amelia and I had talked for nearly four hours. *Four hours!* My husband was not amused, having waited up. Naturally he wanted to know what problem had consumed four hours. I explained that no problem had been verbalized, although I would not have disclosed the details anyway. Privately, I was fairly certain that something dreadful had happened to Amelia during childhood.

My presentations ended at noon on Sunday. Leaving the auditorium, I passed within speaking distance of Amelia and waved. She slowed, her body half turned toward me.

5

"I learned a lot this weekend," she said, before melting into the crowd.

Several years later I returned to the area for a similar speaking engagement. At the morning break I was surprised to run into Amelia. I was even more surprised when she invited me home for a meal afterwards. Having recently married, she wanted me to meet her husband.

At their home, you could cut the tension with the proverbial knife, but I was unable to put my finger on a source. There seemed two levels of communication: one was the overt conscious small-talk; the other, some type of automatic protection program. I recognized the exaggerated startle reflex whenever someone moved too close to Amelia or touched her unexpectedly. I wondered if she'd managed to uncover the source of her rage, which still simmered just below the surface. Recalling her response to my question, "Is your brain angry about something?" however, I held my tongue.

Preparing to return to my hotel, I offered Amelia a scholarship to a weekend seminar on brain function that I presented a couple times each year. She said she'd think about it. At the time I wondered if our paths would ever cross again.

They would.

Over the next couple of decades our paths did cross, several times. I learned that Amelia was getting in touch with her anger and identifying its source. As she shared some of her discoveries with me, one of the first things that jumped out was the completely incompetent parenting she had received.

The Amelia Baker story is not an attempt to validate her recollections. To some degree that has already been done by several therapists. One actually met Amelia at a location of her early childhood. Together they visited a home where Amelia had lived and a ravine where her little brain had recorded some of the most frightening ritualistic activities. The therapist recognized both settings from Amelia's descriptions.

Knocking at the door of one of the houses on the street, the two discovered that the same people still lived there. In turn, the residents recognized Amelia immediately. "Oh, we remember you. Come on it." And the two women went inside.

At the conclusion of the visit, the therapist decided to take another look at the ravine. While walking down the street, she noticed a man exiting the house they'd just been visiting and following at a distance. The therapist, uneasy, chose not to linger.

Amelia saved her drawings from therapy. They are remarkable in that sometimes her conscious memory kicked in only *after* she saw a picture or image emerge on paper, created by her own fingers in front of her own eyes. Selected portions of those drawings have become chapter facings. Some drawings were too gruesome to be included. In fact, parts of Amelia's story itself may be difficult for some to read, and, by her choice, she left out several of the more terrifying episodes.

No book appeals to everyone and not everyone finds everything in any given book helpful or to their taste. In an effort to be as inclusive as possible, however, this book was designed with two goals in mind. The first goal is to present Amelia's story, the *who* and the *what*, if you will. It is told in her own voice without embellishment, embarassment, or whining. She is refreshingly honest in her anecdotes and feelings and their connection to the problems she has had to deal with in adulthood.

 Amelia selected a styalized bird symbol as as metaphor of her life to use at the beginning of each chapter. Helpless as fledglings and easily injured, baby birds can mature into magnificent adults that soar and fly.

The second goal is to provide Chapter Notes for readers who want to increase their knowledge and understanding about topics that surfaced in Amelia's story. This section contains information from relevant emerging research, brain-function studies, and comments by a variety of authors that correlate with Amelia's story. If this is your interest, be sure to read the Chapter Notes.

Refer to the Selected Bibliography for references and other information sources.

This then is the Amelia Baker story—secrets layered upon secrets.

Hear her voice.

Listen and learn.

Remember her story.

—The Authors

Chapter One—
In the Beginning

*Voice is an indicator of self. The loss
of self coincides with a loss of voice in
relationship(s).*

—Dana Crowley Jack

 My name is Amelia Baker and this is my story: a story of secrets layered upon secrets, hidden in a house of silence. For all practical purposes, our house was mostly silent of human conversation.

Yes, I grew up in a house of secrets and a house of silence. I use the word "house" intentionally rather than "home," because it wasn't a "home" in the usual sense. Ideally, home is where the heart lives, where children are nurtured, protected, affirmed, cared for, and taught how to engage in life successfully. That never happened in my family's house. I missed out on that type of parenting.

My parents rarely talked to each other, never mind to me. Well, that's not exactly true. They frequently repeated the family mantra:

> *Our secret. Our secret.*
> *Don't tell. Don't tell.*

When I read an article in the *New York Times* by Sandra Blakeslee, "Studies Show Talking with Infants Shapes Basis of Ability to Think," I thought about my having grown up in a house with so much silence.

According to Blakeslee, "The neurological foundation for problem solving and reasoning are largely established by age one... New studies are showing that spoken language has an astonishing impact on an infant's brain development."

The article points out that some researchers say that the number of words an infant hears each day is the single most important predictor of later intelligence, school success, and social competence. There is one catch—the words have to come from an "attentive, engaged human being."

The words have to come from an attentive, engaged human being. I rarely heard words coming from an attentive engaged human being. I'm not sure I ever experienced that.

I heard *no* words coming from an attentive, engaged human being! Not from my mother, Cookie, and certainly not from my father, Bart. And it wasn't just my mother's inability to parent effectively. My father was silence personified. Every evening and most weekends my parents would sit glued to the television— drinking. They rarely spoke to each other, much less to me, their child.

My father could go for weeks at a time without speaking to either my mother or me. In fact, there was a period of several *months* when, as far as I knew, my parents spoke not one word to each other. I was always caught in the middle of those silent feuds, or disputes, or whatever they were. That's when the silence really screamed.

It would be, "Amelia, tell your father . . ." or "Amelia, tell your mother . . ." Now that's dysfunctional! Those episodes seemed to occur without apparent rhyme or reason.

Talking with infants shapes basis of ability to think. At times I'm amazed that I can speak and write and think as well as I do in adulthood. I sometimes wonder how I might have turned out had I experienced a more normal and nurturing childhood.

The reality is that I didn't and it's an exercise in futility to spend much time on *what ifs.*

I am convinced that part of my early constant humming anger (that I did not even recognize at first and that eventually triggered my getting into therapy) resulted from my lack of effective parenting, along with my puzzlement about the painful events in childhood. My body and my brain must have been living in a constant state of disconnect between what they needed and craved versus what they actually received.

Throughout my entire childhood there was no one with whom I could talk. I might as well have been living in a convent where the sisters had taken a vow of silence, because I lived in a house of silence and a house of secrets. Even if I had known how desperately I needed to get my story out, to talk to someone about what I was experiencing, there was no one safe enough to trust.

I did not choose my parents. I did not even choose my life. I certainly did not choose the abuse—ritual and otherwise. In one sense my story began when I was two years old. In another sense it started four decades later as my life began to unravel, when the secrets layered upon secrets surfaced, when my body rebelled, when my brain remembered, and when the silence screamed.

Everyone's story begins at birth. So did mine. But everyone's story is also a continuation from the previous generation and the one before that and maybe even the one before that. Such was mine. Abuse of many different types was present in my little life, silence being just one of them.

In addition to incest, there were strange ritualistic activities. My mother, her father, and her brother, were involved in ritual groups. I don't know whether my father's family had a similar interest as well. I sense he may have been introduced to ritualistic group activities after he married my mother. I do know that both my father and maternal grandfather were usually present during group ritual activities, and once in a while my mother's brother.

The incidents that caused me the most pain and terror began by the age of two. (At least I have memories from the age of two.) Incidents may have occurred even earlier,  and probably did. Some of my drawings make me think this may be true, although my brain obviously didn't have enough language development to clearly articulate what was happening.

As I said, the unraveling of my life, because of those incidents, would not begin to manifest for decades.

In their book *Ghosts from the Nursery,* authors Karr-Morse and Wiley stress the relevance and long-term impact of early mother-child influences:

> *From the time of late gestation and birth, we begin to develop a template of expectations about ourselves and other people, anticipating responsiveness or indifferences, success or failure. This is when the foundation of who we become and how we relate to others and to the world around us is built. Neurobiology conforms to the environment so that the young brain quickly reflects the cumulative impact of child-parent interactions.*

My child-parent interactions were neglectful, harmful, painful, frightening, confusing, stressful, certainly abusive, maybe even illegal, often non-existent, and definitely downright crazy-making!

> *A moment's insight is sometimes worth a life's experience.*
>
> —Oliver Wendell Holmes

So there was the life I knew consciously, and the life that was hidden from my conscious mind.

My body always knew, however.

It would be a good forty years before my hidden life would awaken.

That would be when the results of chronic stressors and trauma surfaced in my body—unable any longer to keep the secrets hidden. What were those hidden secrets? That's my story.

Stress stimulates the release of the hormones adrenaline, noradrenaline, and cortisol. Unchecked, chronic stress—along with attitudes like hostility, anger, and depression—can lead to sickness and death.

Adrenaline released during stress can stimulate the release of fat cells into the bloodstream. This provides extra energy if it was a real emergency. If not, the liver converts the fat into cholesterol.

—Doc Childre
Freeze Frame

Silent Shadow of Terror

Chapter Two— Down in the Cellar

We can't control what happened; we can't control what has been lost. What we can control is how we fight to take that control back, and the voice within us is powerful in doing so....

—Cathy Gipson

 The house itself wasn't particularly frightening, but the secrets it hid were. And the basement. The basement was terror personified. As a child, I could never identify reasons for the terror. I just knew that even the thought of going down into the basement was enough to trigger an episode of vomiting. Oh, I went into the basement all right, but only with my parents. I was forbidden to go there unless with them. And if they wanted me in the basement, I had to go.

There was no option.

For that matter, it wasn't just our family's basement. The basement in the homes of both my mother's siblings were off limits, as well as that of my maternal grandparents. I was only allowed in the basement if taken there by adults in the family. Eventually, my maternal uncle took over his parents' home. I have very clear memories of that basement, where all the rooms and doors were and where the coal bin was located. Even now if I even think of the coal bin, I get a knot in my stomach accompanied by a sense of overwhelming terror. I cannot explain what it is about the coal bin that triggers those sensations. It just does.

Once when I had just eaten some of my mother's home-baked cookies, something happened to make me think I might have to go down to the basement; that once again I was "in trouble." Although my conscious mind didn't recall what happened in the basement, my body did. Even the thought that I might have to go downstairs triggered a stomach rebellion. It threw up my cookies, literally. And I had loved those cookies.

> *There is an ache in my heart for the imagined beauty of a life I haven't had, from which I had been locked out, and it never goes away.*
>
> —Robert Goolrick

Years later, in therapy, I would begin to understand some of the reasons for my basement fears. Only then would I realize that the terror always involved shaming and humiliation, torture of some type, or death. Some type of payback for an infraction of a rule or a failure to meet expectations.

The basement.

That's where some of my pets had died—or disappeared forever. That's where my beloved cocker spaniel had been dismembered in front of my horrified little eyes, an incident that left a permanent scar on my heart and brain.

The basement.

That's where some of the ritual group experiences had been carried out, where I had experienced abuse by adult members. Standing in a circle, the ritual members would pass me from one to the other, each sexually assaulting me from behind, each then urinating on me, and finally 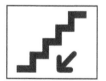 leaving me in a quivering heap on the floor. That's where my father and my maternal grandfather hurt me.

A lot.

And I could not understand.

Our house was uncomfortable. Oh, not in the sense of the house itself. It was uncomfortable in terms of atmosphere: silent, foreboding, stressful. As young as age six or seven, I would do everything in my power to sneak out early on weekends. At daybreak, if possible. My goal was always to get away quickly, quietly, and without waking my parents. I became an expert at opening doors, tiptoeing around, breathing quietly, getting dressed, and doing anything and everything soundlessly.

Sneaking around was not anything to be proud of I suppose, but it is one of the things I learned to do very well—because of my parents. At daybreak or before, I would sneak out with my dog—my only safe friend—and head out to the woods, creeks, trees, meadows, and trails.

I'd lie in the grass, listen to the humming of the insects, watch the clouds and birds overhead, throw sticks for the dog, skip stones in the creek, and walk for hours and hours. I LOVED it! (Still do.) It helped me survive my childhood. I'd stay away all day, returning only when I thought it was an absolute must.

Typically, I would return home only in time for dinner. Upon my return, my parents would act as if they hadn't even noticed I'd been absent the entire day. Indeed, they might not have noticed. Their relationships were with the television, alcohol, aberrant sexual behaviors, and ritual gatherings. Oh, yes, and parties. Their attention was never on me, their daughter, unless it involved sexual abuse or ritual activities.

Were we a happy family in our uncomfortable house? Heavens no! Not in terms of genuine happiness. But I didn't realize that until years later. How can you know what you don't know? When I look at pictures in the family album, some childhood pictures seem happy on the surface. But if it is true that the eyes are the windows of the soul, our eyes were rarely smiling. Mine in particular. In fact it's difficult to find a picture when my eyes mirror any type of genuine happiness. Rather, the windows of my soul appear shuttered, distant, and hesitant.

Certain times of the year were more stressful than others. For example, the summer and winter solstice because at those times for sure there would be ritual gatherings. Although I couldn't identify the reason I dreaded the gatherings, I remembered that I always felt sort of numb and sick for several days afterward. I also recall being in the hospital for several days at a time.

I think that was before the ritual gatherings, not after. Maybe to keep me out of the way during preparations.

Christmas was always another ordeal. Yikes! Talk about over the top! Christmas was way over the top. There were far too many gifts. Embarrassingly so! Even though there were only three of us, there were always heaps and heaps and heaps of  presents. I don't think we were wealthy by any stretch of the imagination, but we certainly weren't poor, either. I have no idea how much money my parents spent. A lot!

I used to wonder if my father were trying to prove that he was a good provider, at least in comparison to his own family who had been dirt poor during his growing up years. Were all the presents to show what a good job *he* was doing?

For my mother's part, it was as if she *had* to buy things to show her love. I must have absorbed some of that at a subconscious level. It's a crazy legacy! I used to feel so smothered by her, and yet I have this urge to buy things for people I care about. Sometimes it drives me nuts, especially during the Christmas season.

At best my presents were a mixed message, as if gifts could make up for the parenting and nurturing I did not receive or for the neglect and abuse I did receive. Were my parents trying to make up for their treatment of me? I'll never know.

I do recall the sense of embarrassment I invariably felt at school when I would hear about the other kids' presents in comparison. There were night-and-day differences in both quantity and quality. I learned quickly to avoid telling the other kids about my presents. If pressed, I'd mention a couple of average items in an off-hand sort of way. I already felt strange and different from those other kids, whose parents usually attended all the sports events, games, and school activities. It was those parents who stood up in the stands and shouted, "Great job, Joe," or "Way to go, Sally," or "We knew you could do it!" Never mine.

At any rate, holidays and ritual seasons were very stressful times. I dreaded them all, if for different reasons. I often became ill around those times, too. Actually, I was a sickly kid for the first decade of my life, having been very underweight at birth, but I think some of that was the constant stress. I was either in terror about something that had just happened or in terror of something dreadful about to happen.

Terror, terror, terror.

Stress, stress, stress.

Most summers our family would go to the beach and stay in a cabin with my mother's parents, sister and/or brother and their spouses. Give them a little time to get unpacked, and they'd start drinking and drinking and drinking, almost nonstop.

One day my father got mad at me for something or other. Grabbing a long section of two-by-four he chased me around the cottage. As I turned the corner, my father slammed the side of the building with the two-by-four. In terror I dove under the cottage for safety, scraping my back badly. My father thought that was terribly funny. He leaned against the porch, laughing and laughing. I, on the other hand, was shivering and shaking, my teeth chattering and clattering. It was hours before I felt safe enough to crawl out from under the cottage.

Years later, when I recalled the cottage incident during a therapy session, my body began to shiver and shake, releasing the terrifying memory it had been hanging on to for all those years. My therapist and I looked around to see what  was making the sound of castanets. There were no castanets.

The sounds came from my teeth chattering and clattering, much as they had during the original incident. Cellular memory, for sure!

Although my father was a very impatient man, he taught me how to drive when I turned sixteen. He even bought me a little sports car. But then (and here's another oxymoron for his parenting), he never asked me any questions. In retrospect, what parent would give their child a little sports car, along with carte blanche to go anywhere at any time of the day or night, no questions asked?

Mine did! I could pack a bag and take off for the weekend and neither parent would ask where I was going, whom I was going with, or when I would return. Most of the time, when I'd would arrive back home Sunday evening (after having been away all day or all weekend), neither my mother nor my father would acknowledge my return in any way, shape, or form. Bizarre. It's like my parents would try to give me experiences but then had no idea how to provide parenting around those experiences. Go figure!

That little car, however, along with hikes in the woods with my dog, now gave me an independence that provided an additional and welcome escape from the silent-screaming house.

While I can't imagine that my parents actually hated me—what child wants to believe that—they were definitely indifferent. That's worse. I have come to believe that the opposite of love is not hate; it's indifference.

During my therapy I remember marveling (and being thankful) that all my away-from-home experiences involved road trips in my little car, playing sports, and similar related activities, rather than choices that were deleterious and destructive.

I grew up taking care of myself, trying as well as I could, but I was not really taught how to do that. Consequently, I am having to learn about balanced self-care in adulthood. Initially, I'd feel guilty for spending any time and money on myself—really guilty—like I didn't deserve either the time or the money. I'm learning, however.

As Parker Palmer put it:

> *Self-care is never a selfish act—it is simply good stewardship of the only gift I have, the gift I was put on earth to offer to others. Because your existence in time and space is unique, there are lives that only you can touch.*

It's interesting. The more I take care of myself, the more energy I seem to have. And the more energy I have, the more I am able to touch the lives of others in positive ways.

And I do have something to offer.

I know that now.

I am a survivor!

In order to escape accountability for his crimes, the perpetrator does everything in his power to promote forgetting. If secrecy fails, the perpetrator attacks the credibility of his victim. If he cannot silence her absolutely, he tries to make sure no one listens.

—Judith Lewis Herman

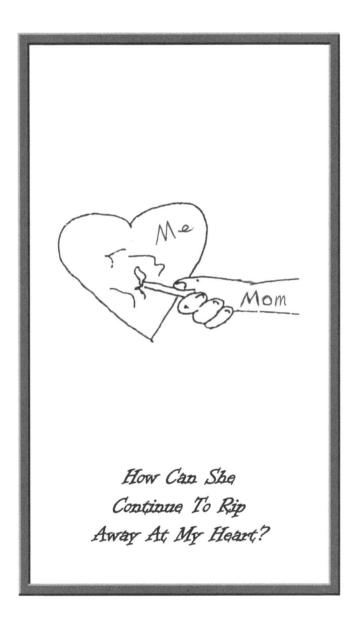

Chapter Three—
Knowledge is Power

Your vision will become clear only when you look into your heart... Who looks outside, dreams. Who looks inside, awakens.

—Carl G. Jung

 The flier advertised a weekend seminar on brain function. Part of me was intrigued. Part of me was stuck in the pattern of avoidance: Don't do anything unless you're sure it's safe. From the moment I had left home at age eighteen, I had selected where I went and who I saw—with care.

Extreme care!

There were very few people I trusted. Precious few. And those few were somewhat superficial acquaintances, at best. No one knew me.

I didn't even know myself!

It was like part of my mind was afraid that sometime, somewhere, I'd come into contact with a person or persons who would run roughshod through something I was trying *not* to remember and alter my carefully crafted and relatively safe life, capsizing the tiny boat that kept me afloat.

Not that I was trying to recall anything, you understand. What was there to recall? In fact, I just wanted to live just in the present moment. Anything that had come before was stuck somewhere in the dim recesses of my subconscious, out of the way.

Brain function? What was *brain function*? Who was this woman? Would she expect me to talk to her? Surely not. No one could try to force me to talk to her, could they? And what would be the purpose anyway? I had nothing to talk about, for heaven's sake! It was all very stressful. But then that was nothing new. My entire life had been one unending string of stressors.

The topic intrigued me, however. I waffled back and forth in my mind: Go? No. Yes. No. I was trying to talk myself out of attending, so it was rather surprising when I actually registered. After all, I reasoned, I could always stay in my room or even leave if I found myself uninterested in the topic.

As the weekend progressed, something about the speaker intrigued me. I found myself watching her: as she spoke, as she walked around the campus, as she interacted with attendees at meals. About noon of the second 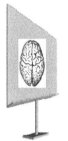 day, I thought: *I'd like to chat with her,* frightening though that thought was! I mean, what would we talk about? Ridiculous. Unsafe.

Nevertheless, at dinner, I found myself moving toward her table and actually ended up asking her if we could chat. She agreed. We would meet in the lounge after the evening presentation. Almost immediately I was kicking myself, metaphorically. However, the deed was done. I keep the appointment.

And when I met with her, the woman had nerve—the colossal nerve—to ask if I knew what my brain was angry about. Angry? Me? Definitely not. I'd felt so upset I'd almost got up to leave. Then she asked whether anything awful had happened to me during childhood. Of course nothing had happened. I'd know if it had, right? The whole idea left me puzzled.

She even had gone on to tell me that there is *usually a valid reason for a brain being angry and that I might want to explore that.* Did I want to explore that? No, I didn't. There was nothing to explore.

I was NOT angry, thank you very much!

Sad, yes. I'd been sad during my entire life.

But NEVER angry.

I did enjoy learning more about brain function, however. It was a fascinating topic. I'd also enjoyed talking with the speaker. Well, most of the time. We'd talked for four hours. *Four hours!* That had to be a record for me. I can't imagine that I had talked to any one person at one sitting for four hours before at least age twenty. Not meaningful communicative conversation. I'd been told what to do often enough, typically in just a few directive sentences, but never in meaningful discussion.

I'd not even had meaningful conversation with my maternal grandmother. She always had candy in her room and often would give me a piece. But I really don't recall her or any of my other grandparents, ever sitting and talking with me like I've since watched other grandparents do with their grandkids. In my case? No reading. No playing. No talking. No joking. I just remember insignificant things like the bowl on the table for spoons. Or the odd dinner times when my maternal grandfather would show me how to eat bread slathered in butter and gravy as dessert.

That brain seminar marked the beginning of the *unraveling*. Of course, I didn't know that then. But it was the start of some internal questioning. Once in a while the thought would flit across my brain: *Was* I angry? My answer was always, "Of course not! What was that woman thinking?" but at least some niggling curiosity existed. My brain and body hadn't yet seriously started kicking up their heels at a level that would get my attention. They would. You can only live life inauthentically for so long before something has to give.

> *Rage can suppress immune system function, raise blood pressure, and place stress on the heart.*
>
> —Helen Fisher, PhD

My brain still has not recalled everything. I know that because once in a while I have a momentary flashback that brings something to conscious awareness. Just a brief flash of terror.

And some of my memories have returned only as fragments, in a sense of anxious foreboding or in profound sadness. My body always knew, however. The remembering was always there, lodged in my very cells, and passed along silently each time they divided. Retained, yet tightly hidden. The problem became that, as my body aged, keeping everything under wraps was more difficult.

All during childhood and for decades in adulthood, I have lived in a constant state of anxiety and apprehension. As a child, I never knew when my parents would take me to the basement or to the ravine where horrible things would happen to me. In adulthood, once I started remembering my history, I never knew when I might be injured. It became a never-ending cycle and resulted in a type of excessive alertness which heightened all my senses.

Because of the chronic stress, my sensory systems were constantly on red alert, Of course that led to sensory burnout. Eventually sight, hearing, taste, smell, and sense of touch actually became less efficient. I still suffer from some of these sensory changes: convoluted sight, limited taste sensations, neuropathy in  places on my shoulders and back, and an inability to tell how hot the water is in the tub or shower.

My physical and mental stress triggered the release of neuropeptides that, in turn, triggered the release of cortisol. High levels of cortisol can damage brain cells and alter brain function. Over time I also developed memory problems and became profoundly depressed, although I didn't realize how depressed. I just thought this was adulthood—Life is hard and then you die.

Now I learned that inadequate amounts of sleep and increased levels of cortisol from chronic stress are associated with abdominal fat, something I have struggled with my entire life. Who knew? I recall being in the doctor's office when I was about age four, having him poke a finger into my soft little dough-boy abdomen and saying to my mother, "You need to watch this or she may struggle with it her entire life." Sure enough. No matter how fit I've been or how much weight I've lost, I can still give the little Pillsbury Dough Boy a run for his money.

Sports became my outlet, to help compensate for the chronic stress. Sports and walking for hours, often with one of my dogs. For years I burned off the anxiety and fear this way. When my body no longer allowed me to do those activities, the dam of emotion and repressed memories began to crack. It would take several more years before the dam finally broke.

Interactions with other human beings—in particular emotional interactions—affect our biological functioning in myriad and subtle ways almost every moment of our lives. They are important determinants of health...

—Gabor Maté, MD
When the Body Says NO

Our Secret. Our Secret.
Don't Tell. Don't Tell.

Chapter Four—
Bathtub to Ravine

Child abuse casts a shadow the length of a lifetime.

—Herbert Ward

 There was always a wooded ravine near our house, no matter where we lived. Each ravine was filled with its own silent shadows.

During childhood, I could never remember the reason I was terrified of the ravine. I just knew that periodically I had to go into the ravine with my parents. For what, I was unsure.

I couldn't recall what happened in the ravine, but when I stood at the edge in memory and looked down into the darkness I would begin to tremble and shake, my teeth literally rattling and chattering.

There were other things that I did remember, and some that I did not want to remember. Whenever those thoughts surfaced, I tried to think of something else, anything else. The baths, for instance. Now those were ugly.

The baths had started in the kitchen sink, one of those partly-good partly-bad experiences that would characterize much of my childhood. Initially, I liked the warm water and the attention from my mother.

If the bath itself was good, the bad part came after. My mother, Cookie, would stand me on the edge of the sink and rub my little body all over with a towel. I would stand there, trembling, a huge sense of dread enveloping me. With my little body all dry, Cookie would stick out her tongue, a big pink tongue. An enormous pink tongue licked at my private parts. Lick, lick, and lick. How I hated that. And as my mother washed and dried and licked, she would chant the family mantra:

> *Our secret. Our secret.*
> *Don't tell. Don't tell.*

(Here, I had to stop writing for a while. My stomach churned too much from the memories—I wonder if that will ever go away—and in retrospect, those were the better of the bathing experiences.)

When I got bigger, my mother would fill the bathtub with hot water, get in and sit at one end, placing me down in the water at the other end of the tub. I would sit there and watch as the water came up high, high, and still higher on my little body. I was fearful I would drown.

Even at that, this was definitely the better part of the bathing experiences. When it was time to get out of the bathtub, my mother would place me flat on the floor. Leaning over me, she would drag her seemingly DD-cup-sized breasts all over my little body. When the soft, squishy breasts came closer and closer to my face, I feared being smothered. It was as if my mother was a huge vortex, like an all-engulfing black hole that sucked me irresistibly into her.

There was no escape. None! But I knew better than to complain or fight. Past experience had already taught me that if I did not acquiesce to whatever my mother wanted, something very bad would happen. I acquiesced. That was preferable to the terror that would envelop me if I didn't.

Sometimes my mother dragged her breasts all over my little body in the basement. At that time, my father would be there, watching and smiling. I never understood the watching and smiling.

When my mother had finished with me, then my father would poke my little body with his erect member. Dragging it across and around and over my body, he would end up at my neck, pressing himself into my throat.

To this day—which now makes sense as to the reason—I cannot wear anything tight around my neck such as turtlenecks, button down shirts, form-fitting collars, or scarfs. Again, I feared being choked or suffocated.

Over and over and over again these activities were acted out until I knew no other. I learned quickly, as a matter of survival, that my body was not my own, that it belonged to these big people who were my parents. These big people with their huge sexual parts, these people who owned me.

And I learned, too, that my body belonged to other adults, as well. Adults who were associates of my parents. My body belonged to those adults, too, with my parents' permission. Some of those adults I knew, and some I didn't. What I did come to know with hopeless certainty was that my body did not belong to me. It belonged to others.

And always the instructions:

Our secret. Our secret.
Don't tell. Don't tell.

And always the silence. Everywhere.

Silence in the ravine, in the basement, in the house—everywhere except for the television. The silence was so silent that it screamed. Much like the terror inside my brain and body.

In therapy I learned that because I was so young and the reality principle had not yet developed in my little brain, illusion and reality were one and the same. I perceived that I must be good. I had to do whatever I was told. If I were bad or refused to acquiesce, something or someone would disappear. A chicken, dog, bird, cat, maybe even another child.

So I did whatever I was told because I truly believed that this would keep something or someone from being hurt or disappearing. Gradually, over the years, I came to believe that my behavior, acquiescing without making a scene, would make the difference between life and death—for someone or something.

Maybe even for me.

Maybe most of all for me.

Add it all together, and the consequence was that I grew up boundaryless.

And because I was boundaryless, I was wide open to invasions of body, mind, spirit, and personal privacy. The end result? I developed profound self-esteem issues.

The years of continued anxiety, stress, and terror, would also take their toll in other ways: in chronic autoimmune diseases, for one.

Karr-Morse and Wiley in *Ghosts from the Nursery* report studies of children under age five who had experienced serious trauma from birth to about age three years. These children appeared to have retained behavior memories. They reenacted the trauma they had experienced in play situations.

Traumatic events may create mental images that can last a lifetime. Some of my past traumatic events came to conscious awareness only after I started drawing whatever came to mind. My body had always remembered; now my brain began to remember consciously through my drawings.

> *Emotional arousal makes any memory stronger. When the memory is of a traumatic experience, persistence can be debilitating.*
>
> —Joseph LeDoux

The day came when I found it both painful and rewarding to realize that my body remembered, had always remembered, had remembered long before my conscious mind was willing or able to recall my traumatic childhood events. It was also both painful and rewarding when I eventually discovered that my brain had remembered, as well.

Perhaps the most disturbing implication from the research on the brain's adaptation to chronic fear and anger is the growing evidence that it may be altering the course of human evolution. Not only can changes in hormone levels be permanent in an individual's lifetime, the altered chemical profile may actually become encoded in the genes and passed on to new generations, which may become successively more aggressive.

—Robin Karr-Morse, Meredith S. Wiley
Ghosts from the Nursery – Tracing the Roots of Violence.

Sucked Into My
Mother's Vortex—Again

Chapter Five—
Naked in Shame

Nothing is predestined: The obstacles
of your past can become the gateways
that lead to new beginnings.

—Ralph Blum

 I remember standing outside our house naked, my four-year-old face pressed into the corner of the porch front steps—cold, unclothed, and ashamed. I knew this had happened because I'd done something wrong or done something to upset my mother, although today I have no idea what that was, and I might not have known back then, either.

Here I was, age four, and my mother had pushed me out the front door with no clothes on, saying that I was to leave and could take only what I had brought with me into the world—which, of course, was nothing. When I look at that picture in my mind's eye, a vague sense of shame still bubbles up.

Shame, because I think the postman and maybe others walked by and saw me standing there, cowering in the corner of the concrete steps. It was more of the crazy-making stuff. My mother, who was supposed to love me the most, shut me out of the house. So I must have done something to deserve that, right? Otherwise a mother would never do that to her child. But what had I done?

I have sometimes wondered what was going on inside our house when I was locked out. Was it something that my mother didn't want me to see? Was Cookie  drunk and simply couldn't be bothered with me at the moment? Was she consciously trying to frighten me so I would be more compliant and acquiescent?

I know that children learn who they are by what is said to them, by what they hear others say about them, and by how they are treated. When a child is pushed outside, naked, and made to stand in full view of anyone walking by, that is a message. When a child is told that if she ever leaves that house, she is to take only what she brought into the world—nothing—that is a message. Those are loud messages of shame and humiliation!

Shame is guilt in overdrive. Shame says "I'm bad, I'm flawed", guilt says "What I did was harmful to myself and/or others, and I can do better than that". Thoughts of healthy, unbiased guilt are how you converse with your conscience, while feelings of shame don't even let the conversation begin.

—Renee Bledsoe

That was me.

Shame-based.

I am aware that this one message probably set me up for a whole host of abandonment issues, along with the abject fear of being unable to take care of myself financially. Certainly, that message has played havoc with me for most of my life. *Take only what you brought with you into the world.* That's likely where my love-hate relationship with money originated, at least partially.

From about age ten, whenever I'd take off to wander in the woods with my dog, I always made sure I had on only whatever clothing I had managed to purchase with my own money. That's likely the reason I got my first job when I was ten, working at a local bowling alley setting pins. I was the only female employee.

Up until age eighteen and living on my own, whenever I left the house, that niggling phrase kept repeating itself inside my head: *Take only what you brought with you into the world.* And this all without even really recalling where that phrase had originated—until I got into therapy.

That message was part of the family script handed to me. Yes, I was handed a script at birth as is everyone else. As my childhood progressed, my parents added instructions to my script, instructions that I had nothing to do with but had to follow in order to survive. I may never uncover all of the instructions in that script. What I am certain of is that I was handed a script at birth and for decades thereafter followed it as if preprogrammed to do so.

> *We all grow up with the weight of history on us. Our ancestors dwell in the attics of our brains as they do in the spiraling chains of knowledge hidden in every cell of our bodies.*
>
> —Shirley Abbott

Part of my recovery involves identifying, reviewing, and tweaking my script so it not only works for me in adulthood but also reflects who I am innately. After graduating from university and while I was teaching, I felt quite secure financially. But when I burned out from teaching, and resigned, no.

That was partly because I had unhealthy boundaries and partly because I eventually became involved with a self-supporting ministry. During those years, with little way to earn a secure and predictable living, I had some recurring physically-frantic episodes of tightening in my chest from financial worries.

Even now, although I have always found a way to take care of myself financially, anxiety circles my heart and squeezes my chest whenever money concerns arise. But it's more than just anxiety. There's also fear, a fear that at some point I am going to end up living on the streets. Maybe not naked as in my childhood but perhaps as some type of bag lady.

It has become a bit of a joke with a couple of my friends who know me well. They chuckle when I get into a frantic panic over money. Usually I say something silly such as, "I need to be sure to get a *big* shopping cart in case I end up homeless and living on the street."

Although they don't know all the details of my history and don't realize where those fears originated, they remind me that it is highly unlikely I'll ever be a bag lady. Their affirmations haven't stopped the anxiety attacks, however.

Whenever my brain becomes anxious, it tends to direct its attention and energy toward the middle brain layer. Automatically, I *downshift* into the subconscious, emotionally-reactive limbic system. That's where panic attacks live, where phobias hide. And I can get a panic attack in nothing flat, in a nanosecond!

Thinking about my living on the street as a bag lady may have been a *bit of a joke* to my friends, but it is no joking matter for me. It was no laughing matter during childhood, either. Just thinking about standing naked outside brings back feelings of humiliation and shame for being unclothed, terror for being locked out of the house, and so much confusion because I had no idea what in the wide-wide world I had done to warrant such treatment. It's all part of my trying to make sense of the nonsense. But there's no making sense of the nonsensical.

> *Shame-humiliation dynamics always accompany child abuse. If synapses are never built due to neglect, or destroyed by stress neurochemicals, the individual may be left without the ability to connect, trust, or experience empathy (e.g., extreme instances may result in sociopathy).*
>
> —Robin Karr-Morse, Meredith S. Wiley

Through it all, I was expected to be seen and not heard. Better yet, not even be seen. In order to follow the family script that had been handed to me, I had to give up my own voice and develop a pattern of living in isolation. I had to do whatever the adults wanted me to do. I had to learn to live with pain, shame, terror, confusion, and a demeaning self-image. I was expected to buy into the thought patterns of the adults in my little world. I could not think for myself.

> *With a good script, a good director can produce a masterpiece. With the same script, a mediocre director can produce a passable film. But with a bad script even a good director can't possibly make a good film.*
>
> —Akira Kurosawa

The pictures that I drew for my therapists showed all manner of scary things: altars, hoods, long robes, knives, blood, and objects that involved animals and birds and pets. Perhaps because my childhood involved so much terror, some of those sketches show just my eyes peeking out through a wall or a coat of armor. In order to feel safe in adulthood, I developed an overwhelming need to know what was happening around me at all times. Unless I knew, I was jumpy and restless, not the best model for developing friendships with other human beings.

Even today, my first reaction in most situations is still to assume that I am in trouble for something. As far as I know, I rarely dissociate any more—split off a group of mental processes or ideas from my main body of consciousness. I can downshift in a nanosecond, exhibiting an out-of-proportion anxiety response or overreaction. Sometimes this is for fear of upsetting the other person— and risk being "in trouble."

For example, if the phone rings while company is visiting, I may hear myself say, "Is it okay if I answer the phone?" rather than just making my own decision about whether or not to take the call. I still struggle with a need for permission to engage in simple, every-day actions for fear of annoying the other person.

> *Family scripts are revealed when repeating patterns of family interactions are either observed or described.*
>
> —John Byng-Hall

Close friends have pointed out that I can flip–flop almost instantly from a state of being over-concerned to a response of "I don't care." I'm working on this. My guess is that this pattern developed as a self-preservation strategy to prevent me from feeling too deeply. I now recognize that it can kick in when my anxiety is on the rise or becomes too overwhelming.

I compare it to a form of walking on eggshells (which is what I did, especially around my father). At any rate, I grew up with a hidden but seething slush fund of unresolved emotions that eventually began to pop out periodically in the form of very inappropriate anger—usually a serious overreaction. My anger was inappropriate for what was going on at the time in the environment, but the overreaction was not surprising considering the abuse I had experienced during childhood.

One way I know that my recovery is working has to do with the awareness of my anger. It surfaces now when I perceive my personal boundaries are being invaded. I recognize it much more quickly and express it much more appropriately.

Once two systems come in energetic contact, they are connected forever by the infinite cellular memory of their connection. Our experiences with parents and others close to us remain within us. Cellular memory is a form of energy. As with matter, energy is not destroyed so information stored at the cellular level is retained indefinitely.

—Paul Pearsall, PhD

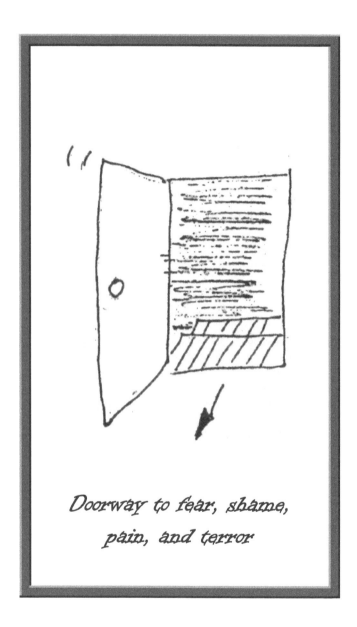

Doorway to fear, shame, pain, and terror

Chapter Six—
Elephantine
Dysfunction

*People talk about 'dysfunctional'
families; I've never seen any other
kind.*

—Sue Grafton

 My parents met when my mother went into a business establishment where my father worked and asked to open an account. When" she told him her name was Cookie, my father made some joke about that. Eventually they began dating, became engaged, and married. The service took place in an Anglican church, as my father's family was Anglican.

When my parents married, my mother's name became Cookie Baker. My father thought that was funny and often teased my mother.

"Cookie Baker! Cookie Baker!" he'd say and laugh. They had BBC embroidered on their towels. Again, my father thought that was hilarious. "BBC!" he would say, teasingly. "BBC! No, not the British Broadcasting Company; just Bart Baker (and) Cookie."

Some people tend to throw around the term "dysfunctional family" with abandon. I never heard that term when I was a child. From the perspective of adulthood, I now realize that my family was dysfunctional. Very dysfunctional, with a capital 'D!' While growing up, however, that's all I knew. Dysfunctional was our *normal.* In adulthood, obviously that did not serve me well. Even with therapy, learning new behaviors has always been a challenge. And I needed to learn a lot of new behaviors!

My mother was the eldest of three children, having a younger brother and sister. Unlike my father, my mother wasn't athletic. She couldn't even swim. She would try sports activities but none seemed to work for her. She could cook, bake, sew, and knit. She even had a little artistic side to her. She did a few paint-by-number pictures when those kits first came out and even did some work with copper. However, from all of that, she taught me very little of anything that was positive.

At least very little that I can recall.

I'd like to believe that my parents loved each other, really loved each other, at least initially. Most children probably wish that. I guess I'll never know for sure. I do know I saw precious little evidence of *love* in their behaviors toward each other. Or toward me, for  that matter. They certainly didn't make a habit of hugging and kissing each other. Nor did they make a habit of hugging and kissing me in the way I saw other parents do when they picked their kids up after school. I never remember being hugged or kissed by either parent simply because I was their daughter.

When my mother did kiss me, it felt strange and creepy. Growing up, I never liked her. Eventually I figured it out—not until much later, however. Cookie was the one who always "loved" me. She

> *The further backward you look, the further forward you can see.*
>
> —Sir Winston Churchill

smothered me with a weird (to me) type of affection that was very uncomfortable. I hated it and hated her. It was worse when she was drunk. Then she wanted to hug me or kiss my cheek, and I would just turn my head or say no.

The worst was when she was sexually abusing me. I always felt "slimed" by my mother, like being sucked into a vortex of licking, kissing, touching, rubbing, and hugging. Sometimes I felt as if she had shoved something sharp right into my little heart.

And always the anger—although I did not know that's what it was—releasing adrenalin and dopamine to keep me going. Anger, fear, and silence. That was my life. An endless cycle of anger, fear, and silence.

In retrospect, my mother was very needy. Maybe that was why she turned to alcohol. I often wonder whether the alcohol was because she craved love or because of her history with rituals or the sexual abuse she orchestrated. Likely some of each.

I've learned that hurting people often hurt other people.

I simply cannot comprehend a parent doing to a child what my mother did to me, at least not without the parent suffering some level of guilt. On the other hand, similar things may have been done to her during her childhood. People often tend to repeat what was done to them. It may have been all she knew and, for some reason, either refused or was unable to perceive it as unhealthy, dysfunctional, and abusive.

Typically we celebrated my father's birthdays—at least the milestone numbers such as 50, 60, 65, 70, and 80—with a party. For some reason we never celebrated my mother's birthdays. Never. My mother was never really celebrated in any special way, except perhaps a card at Mother's day; yet she was the one who remembered everyone else's birthday, buying gifts, preparing meals, baking cakes, and so on. My mother wanted so much to be accepted and appreciated, but her sloppy, smothering, often 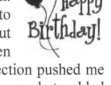 drunken efforts to win my affection pushed me further and further away. Too much troubled water had flowed under the proverbial bridge.

In my later adult years I came to pity my mother. She was trying so hard to win love with her cooking being so "empty" from the lack of love in her life. It's only my speculation, but I think she was giving out of the deep well of her own unmet needs in an effort to feel better about herself.

The one and only time I had a surprise party for my mother's birthday, I used my grandmother as an excuse to get my mother to come home. For a time my mother owned a "smoke and gift" shop. On this occasion, I called the shop and told my mother to come home immediately because grandmother wasn't doing well.

My mother rushed home crying and asking what was wrong. I felt badly having used my grandmother as a false excuse to get my mother home. But I didn't know how else to get her there.

When my mother finally realized I had planned a surprise party for *her* birthday, she started really crying in earnest. It turned out okay in the end, and I was glad I had done something nice for her. But later on I was puzzled about my even having wanted to plan the surprise birthday party. Wherever had that come from?

It was all such a confusing and stressful mixed bag. Part of me wanted to make my parents happy; part of me did not because I was so unhappy.

When a child grows up in a dysfunctional environment, among primarily dysfunctional behaviors, the observed patterns can begin to seem normal.

> *Everybody is a genius. But if you judge a fish by its ability to climb a tree, it will spend its whole life believing that it is stupid.*
>
> —Albert Einstein

For example, you've probably heard the expression: the elephant in the room. Author Stephen King talks about that. He wrote:

There's a phrase, the elephant in the living room, which purports to describe what it's like to live with a drug addict, an alcoholic, an abuser. People outside such relationships will sometimes ask, "How could you let such a business go on for so many years? Didn't you see the elephant in the living room?" And it's so hard for anyone living in a more normal situation to understand the answer that comes closest to the truth; "I'm sorry, but it was there when I moved in. I didn't know it was an elephant; I thought it was part of the furniture." There comes an aha-moment for some folks, the lucky ones, when they suddenly recognize the difference.

 Eventually, I began to recall the outline of an *elephant* in *our* living room.

I also recalled hearing the words: *My brain's opinion is that yours is very angry.*

Remembering that sentence made the possibility of my digging into the past seem less about me and more about my brain, a slightly less daunting prospect.

And, as angry behaviors surfaced more and more frequently in my life, I actually began to wonder about the source of that anger.

And there were also the words: *There is usually a valid reason for a brain being angry. You might want to explore that.*

Those words helped depersonalize my curiosity and make the journey of exploration seem doable. Well, almost. Eventually, the pain and the curiosity, the anger and the depression, blended to the point that I risked taking a good look at my brain's anger, risked searching for a valid reason, risked finding and using my voice.

I now perceive the truism in the phrase: *Every pathology has an ecology.* Dysfunctional behaviors do not arise out of a vacuum. There is something in the environment that serves as a trigger.

Many of your attitudes, perceptions, and emotional responses are deeply ingrained in your cellular patterning. Your nerve cells store and retain accumulated memories of past and present emotionally charged events.

—Doc Childre and Howard Martin
The HeartMath Solution

No Escape
Horror
Terror Personified

Chapter Seven—
Party On!

*Feelings of worth can flourish only in
an atmosphere where individual
differences are appreciated, mistakes
are tolerated, communication is open,
and rules are flexible—the kind of
atmosphere that is found
in a nurturing family.*

—Virginia Satir

 Nothing in my life matched Satir's description of a nurturing family.

Absolutely nothing!

Speaking of *family*, information about my father's family is a bit murky. I know that my father, Bart Baker, was the youngest child but could never get a firm handle on the actual number of children in the family. Reportedly the family included one sister, a male cousin who grew up with them, and several brothers.

A couple of his brothers supposedly died before they reached the age of two, at least one of whom was killed by being run over by a wagon (as the story goes). I recall meeting or hearing about three living brothers, but the stories were never very clear or consistent.

Interestingly, my paternal grandparents were cousins with the same last names. This meant that Baker married Baker; my grandmother never changed her name. In one way that was simple; in another it was confusing. No wonder it was murky!

The family was dirt poor. So poor in fact that Bart and his siblings would go out to the nearby railway tracks, to collect hot coals that fell from trains, and bring the hot embers back to the house for cooking and keeping warm.

Because his family had been extremely poor, in adulthood my father worked hard to provide material things for my mother and me. Our family always had a nice house, a car, and often extras like a swimming pool. For whatever reason, this didn't extend to providing quality parenting, emotional nurturing, or affirmation.

When Bart returned from military service, he became a traveling salesman. I was born several years after his return.

My mother had been pregnant several times before I was born with at least two viable children. Both reportedly died soon after birth, one of whom had hydrocephalus.

I always wondered if any of those pregnancies had involved twins. My maternal grandmother was a twin; my mother's brother had a set of  twins. I wasn't particularly interested in having children of my own, no surprise at all.

When I did think about the twins that seemed to run in our family, however, I wondered if I might have had twins—had I wanted children.

Speaking of children, I was told that I had four sisters, none of whom were alive. Apparently this information was not disseminated to extended family members because years later when I asked about my mother's pregnancies or gravesites, these family members acted as if this was all new information. I have no proof, but my clear impression was that my mother was a breeder for the rituals. Again, I have no proof, but I grew up with the clear sense that I was being groomed to take her place.

With my mother's reported history of miscarriages, who knows what her mindset and mental attitudes were during my in utero experience.

At birth I was a very small baby, so tiny I was placed in an incubator and fed with an eyedropper. I was a somewhat sickly child and I seemed to catch every illness and disease going around. Until at least age eight, I was sick most of every winter.

Both my parents had a tight relationship. Unfortunately it was with alcohol rather than with me or each other. Next to drinking alcohol, they loved hosting parties, often around holidays and especially at the New Year.

At parties, Bart and Cookie could be counted on to chat and socialize, and, of course, drink. There would be lots of people, lots of smoking, lots of drinking, lots of music, lots of dancing, and lots of gaiety. It was always my job to empty all the ashtrays the morning after a party. Yuk.

From my earliest conscious memory, I knew my dad drank. I also knew he'd get *happy* after a few beers, and I liked it when he was happy. At least he would talk! And sometimes he would sing—he had a good tenor voice and was quite musical—but only at parties. I remember many times as a kid when we'd visit my mom's family (many of whom were musical), my aunt would play the piano.

We'd all have spoons to keep rhythm and sometimes the guitar and drums could come out as well. We'd would sing for hours at a time. I especially watching my dad sing. I can still picture him standing by the piano, cigarette in one hand, beer bottle in the other, and a huge smile on his face. He'd raise his head and sing like a lark on a branch. It was the only time I ever saw my father really joyful and laughing. In some ways, those were the magical times. It never lasted, however, that joy. And I never saw it exhibited outside of a party environment.

Much of my talent appears to actually have come from my often silent and distant father. He wrote poems, loved to sing, and possessed a goodly amount of musical ability. He bought me an accordion and gave me a few lessons. But he never encouraged me to practice, set any expectations for practice, or showed any interest in my progress. Without that, my interest died away.

Since I inherited some musical ability from my father, I've tried my hand at everything from accordion, piano, guitar, harmonica, and kazoo, to spoons. To date I haven't yet found anything that feels right for me to express music, other than my whistling, that is. When I was around age eight or nine, my aunt wrote a little verse about me and music.

It went like this:

> *There's music in the kettle,*
> *There's music in the spout*
> *There's music in Amelia—*
> *But it won't come out*

My music does come out in whistling, and people often make comments (and much-appreciated affirmations) such as, "I like the way you whistle," or "I wish I could whistle like that."

I do have one really positive musical memory about my father from a time when I was probably about age twelve or thirteen. I came home from school one day to find him in a good mood. Silently, without saying what he was doing, my father proceeded to line up a group of empty beer bottles on the kitchen counter. Then he filled them with varying levels of water. I watched silently, fascinated.

When the beer bottles were filled to his satisfaction, he blew across their tops to make sounds. Soon I began to do the same and before long we were blowing and actually playing a melody—the national anthem, as I recall. Blowing and playing, playing and blowing. It only happened that once, but the experience remains one of my very few "happy memories."

At a party, my dad was usually the last to call it a night, and mostly with my mom's brother. The two would sit up "discussing" into the wee hours of the morning. In my early twenties, while visiting home, I heard a *kafuffle* (our family word for something unusual) in the hall.

My aunt and my mom were helping my father crawl from the living room to the bathroom. He was far too drunk to find the way on his own, let alone stand. They were talking with each other in whispers, hoping I wouldn't hear him and them. When they finally got him to the bathroom, my dad peed all over the floor, and my mom and aunt cleaned up the mess. At first I was both furious and embarrassed. And then, for the first time, I remember consciously deciding to no longer feel shame about my father's drinking. That was HIS behavior.

My father came by his love of alcohol honestly—parents, grandparents, and likely great, as well, were heavy drinkers. My paternal grandfather's modus operandi would be to pick up his paycheck, grab the boys, go to a bar, and spend the entire sum on liquid refreshment. Not every male in my father's line remained alcoholic, however. One of my dad's brothers "got religion" and quit drinking. He became rather morose and addicted to religiosity, something like the description of a *dry drunk.*

That suggests that addictive behaviors of more than one type ran through the generations of my family. For sure, my parents drank every day. Typically my father began drinking as soon as he got home from work. He preferred beer and would usually consume a six-pack at a minimum. He'd begin with a beer or two or three before dinner. Then he'd have one or two more with dinner and a couple more after dinner. He could usually handle beer tolerably well. But just let him start drinking hard liquor, and he'd become drunk very quickly.

My father was the quintessential Dr. Jekyll and Mr. Hyde. He might be in one of his don't-speak-to-the-family moods, but just let some guest drop by the house and instantly Bart would become Mr. Personality—talkative, outgoing,  witty, pleasant, funny, and pouring booze—the perfect host. Whenever friends or family dropped by, the booze would flow like a wide river. Give him a few drinks and my father would turn into this devil-may-care almost charismatic host. He would be a happy drunk, the *life of the party*. People loved it! Then the company would leave and my father would go back to not speaking to anyone in the family: silence personified. He probably wasn't two different personalities literally, but he certainly was in terms of exhibited behaviors.

I learned to recognize quite quickly when my father was *really* drunk because he'd start to philosophize. He'd get into a "discussion" with me or my uncle, actually more like "quiet arguments." And my dad COULD NOT be wrong. Eventually I'd go to bed. Nevertheless, even those so-called philosophical discussions, were basically welcome. At least it was conversation and much better than the uncomfortable, cold, impenetrable silence which was the norm for our household.

My mother, on the other hand, drank rye. She would become gushy, mushy, sloppy, and slurry when drinking. How I hated that. Sometimes during my teaching years, my mother would phone when she'd been drinking, and it was all I could do to be civil. Sometimes I was impatient and not very polite.

I could never discover enough about my mother's generational inheritance to know if she came by her love of rye through example and cellular memory or because she was trying to forget the myriad dysfunctions in her life and marriage.

I knew that both her parents were teetotalers but what of their parents and grandparents? Did they drink?

It would have been unthinkable to ask.

That was another oxymoron, because if anyone wanted to be proud of me, it was my mother. I never felt like hers was a genuine pride in my accomplishments, however. Rather, it was all about her identity: "This is *our* daughter, a teacher, and a national athlete." It was all about how good *they* looked because of *my* accomplishments. Their pride and joy in me was all in public, especially at parties.

Inside the walls of our house, it was another story entirely. My perception was that my parents didn't give two hoots about me as an individual. They just used me for their own ends.

I remember one Christmas in adulthood when I purchased airline tickets and surprised my parents with a holiday visit. While individually they seemed glad to see me, they were in one of those no-talk-to-each-other periods of time. And, of course, they were drinking and drinking and drinking. (Based on their drinking patterns, I think it safe to conclude that both my parents would definitely qualify as alcoholic.)

Later I recall asking myself: "Why did you spend all that time, money, and energy on the visit? What was the purpose? Were you hoping against hope that this time it would be different?"

Of course, it never was different!

My father had a complex relationship with my mother, one I could never really figure out. My mother was clearly in charge of all ritualistic activities. At times, my father appeared to be in charge, but that was an illusion. His activities were always under my mother's direction, which might have been part of the reason he drank every day or that gradually he stopped interacting with us.

Inside the house, the silence was deafening.

My mother's identity was wrapped up in her cooking, so wrapped up she could never take 'no' for an answer when she offered food. No matter how full I was, my mother would put *just a little more* on my plate. Either that or she would exhibit some passive-aggressive maneuver, emitting a little moan of disappointment or putting on a sad facial expression if I didn't want any more to eat.

Both my mother and grandmother went through periods of being very overweight. It's amazing I didn't end up obese! At Cookie's funeral, I actually had to chuckle because the people who reminisced about my mother uniformly mentioned her dinners, especially her Yorkshire pudding and lemon pie.

One morning I entered the kitchen during one of my father's don't-speak-to-the-family episodes, those long silent periods of time during which he would say absolutely nothing whatsoever to any of us. My mother was fixing breakfast. Seeing me, she said, "Good morning."

I responded with a grunt, mimicking one of my father's typical behaviors.

"You know," my mother said, "you don't have to be like your father. You can choose to be cheerful in the morning."

What a concept! I thought about her words and from then on, I tried to be more upbeat. In adulthood, my friends have often commented about my morning cheerfulness. I tell them, "Cheerfulness is a choice. One positive behavior that I actually learned from my mother."

So, in spite of all of the dysfunction, I did manage to develop at least one positive characteristic. That realization has been helpful as I view my childhood through adult eyes and develop a positive mindset. I am grateful for learning that cheerfulness is *good medicine*.

It surely is!

Our past experience was imprinted in our data base. We will repeat our parents' behaviors until we remove the program. Before we can have successful relationships and become successful parents we must unload our garbage that is setting us up to perpetuate our parents' parenting model—with all its dysfunctional behavior patterns.

—Art Martin, PhD

Help! Somebody Help!
I'm Trapped!

Chapter Eight—
Kept in the Dark

Childhood trauma does not come in one single package...trauma does not have to occur by abuse alone.

—Dr. Asa Don Brown

As I write and watch my story emerge on paper, it has become increasingly clear how very isolated I felt growing up. I really don't remember having any childhood friends nor do I recall other children coming to our house to play.

I remember often being in the out of doors, usually alone except for my pets. When I did come in contact with other children outside of a school setting, those encounters—if observed by my mother—typically resulted in my being punished in some way or another. Again, I could never figure out what rules I had broken or what I had done to displease her.

One time I met the little neighbor boy through the fence that separated our properties. I taught him how to get out of his yard. (I wonder now the reason he felt *he* had to escape.) When that was discovered, I was tied up in a harness on the front porch. Everyone going by the house could see me tied up. My mother even put the harness on backwards so I couldn't untie it. Talk about more shame!

Another time I met a little girl who I recognized from a basement experience. I must have felt an overwhelming wave of empathy for her, because I ran over and gave her a hug. Not a good choice because my mother saw me do this, and I got into a great deal of trouble for that spontaneous action. A great deal of trouble!

By *trouble* I mean that it led me to a trip down into the basement. That punishment probably helped set me up for honing skills of dissociation and pushed me toward building walls of isolation, boundaries that were almost impenetrable.

> *Whenever the going gets too rough, we need to leave our bodies in order to lessen the intensity of what we are feeling.*
>
> —Christine Caldwell (on dissociation)

Our family was relatively isolated, as well. My mother phoned her parents regularly, so there must have been some attachment there. She had grown up a practicing Catholic, as had members of her family for several generations back. Through family-of-origin work, I was able to verify that my mother's family appeared to have been involved in ritual activities for a generation or two back. (I found no evidence of such with my father's family.) Obtaining this piece of information helped me stop trying to "make sense of the nonsensical," as I have come to think of it, and also helped me realize that my mother just passed along what in all likelihood had been done to her.

Sometimes my maternal grandparents would come to our house for Christmas dinner. I never recall going to their place for holiday dinners. Ever. Once in a while we visited my mother's brother and sister and their families, and occasionally they visited us on holidays. Visits were sporadic, however.

In adulthood when I asked my uncle about the inconsistency of family get-togethers, he replied that my father's *wandering hands* had made a pass at my aunt. Those wandering hands definitely had not been well received. Whether or not we saw members of my mother's extended family depended on whether or not family members were talking to each other. More patterns of silence.

So we were isolated and yet we were not isolated. That was the ongoing oxymoron. When I was about seven, my parents began taking in foster children, usually older teenagers. They came and went and came and went like a revolving door. I remember one of the girls was always mad at my father. I wish I knew what that was all about. Was it another "wandering hands" situation? And then the foster children disappeared, one or two at a time, and I never got to say goodbye.

 My father's family was Anglican. After my parents married, when my mother became involved with any church-related activities, it was always with the Anglican Church. She taught knitting to groups of seven-year-old girls (my age), all in green uniforms. I had no uniform neither did I ever get to play with those girls.

About that time my father built a small apartment in our basement for my mother's parents. While they lived with us, my mother's relatives regularly came to visit them every Sunday. There were some fun family times with them: skating on the pond, sliding down hills on the toboggan, and playing in the creek. As usual, there was a lot of drinking. Once, during one of those Sunday-drinking binges, my father and my mother's brother put pajamas on my pony, Tiny. My pony disappeared later on, too. Once more, I was in the dark!

My mother's father was diagnosed with colon cancer that metastasized throughout his body. I visited him in the hospital, once. That's my first recollection of being told that a person was dying. When he did die, as a Catholic, there was a large Catholic funeral. The service included priests, altar and candles, choir boys, incense, and the whole nine yards. I was mesmerized by the pageantry because our family attended church very irregularly.

I was totally shocked (still am) at the response of my mother to her father's death. At one point, while her father was being viewed, the funeral home closed off the family from the rest of the attendees. My mother literally draped herself over her father in the casket, and both she and my great uncle cried and sobbed and wailed! It was totally frightening, since our home was basically emotionless and silent. I'd never seen such a display of emotion. It was overwhelming!

My parents never told my maternal grandmother that her husband had died. More silence! By then, she had had several strokes, had lost the ability to speak, and was somewhat unaware. She continued to live with us until her death. I remember she always had jam smeared on her glasses. Earlier in life she had been very heavy, but after she died and they took her out on the gurney, I could see only her head and toes, she was so small.

My mom cried a little, but it no big deal as when her father had died. I did not attend my grandmother's funeral. I certainly hadn't enjoyed my grandfather's and had no idea if my mother's behavior would again be as over the top. I just knew I didn't want to repeat that experience! My parents didn't seem to mind either way. This meant that I don't know for certain if my mother fell apart as she had done at her father's funeral. I doubt it. What was interesting, in retrospect, was that my mother never mentioned her parents again. Never.

We were very isolated from my father's parents, so I have few memories. I do recall that my paternal grandpa had a funny chin. He would take his teeth out and have me try, and try, and try to touch my nose to my chin like he could. That was funny. Apparently he was violent with my grandmother and would hit her. He'd get drunk and spend all his pay at the local bar. He'd take off, frequently, too, for short and long periods of time, leaving her behind to raise the kids. No wonder Grandma eventually did laundry, took in boarders, and worked really hard to make ends meet.

I remember my father's mother as a stern woman and rarely saw her smile. I think she must have been a stoic, just keeping on keeping on. When she could no longer live alone, Grandma came to live with us. I remember she had a big spring-loaded hypodermic needle.

She used that syringe every night to give herself an insulin injection. I also remember that she would take her teeth out and put them in a glass by her bed before going to sleep. As a kid, I found that very interesting and amusing.

I wasn't told when she died. She just silently disappeared from our lives. I was not informed of my paternal grandfather's death, either. He just disappeared, too, but because we hardly ever saw him, it didn't faze me. I don't recall seeing any evidence of grief in either of my parents when my paternal Grandpa and Grandma disappeared, but I certainly knew to not ask any questions. As with my maternal grandparents, no one mentioned my father's parents again. More silence.

> Any type of threat can trigger the brain to downshift. A threat is anything that triggers a sense of helplessness in the individual.
>
> —Renate N. Caine
> Geoffrey Caine

When my therapist asked about the predominating atmosphere during my childhood, fortunately I had progressed beyond my earlier perception of coming from a happy, idyllic family. This time I didn't even have to think about it. I answered immediately: *Foreboding.* I had lived my entire childhood in an atmosphere of foreboding, a fearful anxiety, a hovering silent threat, a sense of being in trouble for doing something wrong.

I never could figure out exactly what I was doing or had done wrong, you understand, but that never stopped me from trying even harder to be good and to meet expectations.

That fearful anxiety, however, probably keep me downshifted most of my childhood. I learned that the natural brain phenomenon of downshifting is often triggered by fear, by feeling unsafe. As Carolyn Poole put it, when people feel threatened they downshift: feel helpless, don't look at possibilities, don't feel safe to take risks or challenge old ideas, and have limited choices for behavior.

Much later in life I remember reading a quote that helped me get a much better handle on downshifting:

I have had control issues all my life,
especially as more abuse issues
surfaced... When I notice my controlling
behavior, I ask myself what I'm afraid
of and get to the root of the fear. Facing
the origins of the fear helps me gain my
power back instead of using control as
an illusion of empowerment.

—Christina Enevoldsen

Downshifting happens so quickly that I often recognize it only after it's already happened.

Nevertheless, I continue to learn strategies not only to help me recognize when my brain has downshifted but also to prevent unnecessary downshifting. I am using these tools to help my brain upshift, to move from the emotionally reactive subconscious layers up into the conscious-thought layer.

These are key recovery pieces.

As they say, you can only get out of a trap once you recognize you're in one. Awareness is the first step.

An increasing awareness of my own behaviors against the backdrop of emerging brain-function information has influenced me significantly. I believe it helped save my life.

Downshifting occurs when the individual detects threat in an immediate situation and full use of the great new cerebral brain is suspended, while faster-acting, simpler brain resources take larger roles. The degree of downshifting reflects the degree of threat as perceived by the individual.

—Leslie A. Hart
Human Brain and Human Learning

Shame!
Terror!
Anxiety!

Chapter Nine—
Nonsensical Nonsense

*Anxiety is love's greatest killer. It
makes others feel as you might when a
drowning man holds on to you. You
want to save him, but you know he will
strangle you with his panic.*

—Anaïs Nin

 We moved like clockwork at least once every couple of years for as far back as I can remember. There was never any rational explanation for our many moves. We'd just get settled into a house and it was time to move again. So there was always some level of anxiety because nothing ever seemed permanent.

As I began to write about some of the activities that took place in the basement of our houses or in the nearby ravines, I logged the moves. I also logged the times when my dogs and cats and pony had mysteriously gone *missing*.

I thought about Preemie (a cocker spaniel and my absolute favorite) and Buddy, Sally and Tag, Scamp and Pug, Cindy and Mitzy, and  there were many more. We usually had at least two dogs at any one time. That way when one dog went "missing" I still had the other. One would disappear, then be replaced. Once I went with my father to the animal pound and he picked out a dog to bring home. At other times a dog would vanish, and then a replacement would show up, and so on.

One day I returned home from school, and my dog Cindy was missing. My mother said my father had put out rat poison, and Cindy had eaten some. But my father never said he was sorry about the rat poison. And neither of my parents ever mentioned Cindy again. She was just gone.

And then there were the cats: Twinkle and Fez, Muffy and Smokey and Snowball, among others. When Muffy disappeared my mother said my dad ran over the cat, but I never saw that happen and my father never mentioned it. Not even once. And where *was* Muffy? The cat wasn't in the garbage can. Did someone *bury* Muffy? There was no mound in the garden. There were never any fresh mounds.

As one by one my pet dogs and cats disappeared, I would ask where they were. Usually there was no response whatsoever from my parents, and I know for certain neither of them ever helped me look for the missing creature.

Silence again. Strange.

My mother orchestrated all the rituals. Even when my father, my mother's brother, and my maternal grandfather were present, she was clearly the one in charge. That has always puzzled me because on the surface she wasn't a strong or dominant personality.

I remember that the ritual-group members included at least a doctor, a nurse, and a policeman. Any one of them could take a kid to the hospital for treatment, no questions asked. During those rituals, I was usually sexually abused by my father, maternal grandfather, and other male neighbors and friends who were members of the group.

Sometimes when I didn't want to do what they wanted in a ritual, my mother would come over to me and say, "Just do what they want." I remember trying to dig my heels in, and my grandfather just pushing me back toward the center of the circle. And again, my mother telling me to just do whatever he wanted.

My mother! My own mother!

The rituals took place several times each year like clockwork, including the winter and summer solstice. Typically the ritual gatherings were held either in our basement or in a nearby ravine. I can recall being forced to observe or participate in at least twenty-three ritual events.

During childhood I was certain I would never live to be over age twenty-five. Back then I had no conscious reason for that perspective. I just "knew." And then I recall being astonished when just I kept on having birthdays.

According to author Margaret Smith (a pseudonym), ritual abuse is the most terrifying as well as the most underestimated form of child abuse. I believe my experiences set me up to live in fear. I've lived in a constant state of anxiety from as far back as I can remember— and that's pretty far back now that I have more yesterdays than tomorrows. A sense of sadness and loss often alternated with states of anxiety and terror.

Actually, in retrospect, I lived in a continual state of mild, all-pervasive dread.

And I always *ALWAYS* felt isolated, alone, and unloved.

I have lived my life for decades in a state of hypervigilance, as well. Even to this present time I struggle not to let it take over. I constantly feel like I'm being watched or that I must explain myself or that I will have to defend myself over something. Intellectually, I realize that I am now an adult and can protect myself. Emotionally, it's a different matter.

That hypervigilant startle reflex can kick in within a nanosecond, especially if I'm touched by someone unexpectedly or by someone I don't trust or in any manner whatsoever that reminiscent of the many unwanted touches I was forced to accept and tolerate in childhood. I find that I'm especially vulnerable if someone comes up behind me and touches me. It's as if my brain instantaneously connects the present with the past and brings all the weight of that grief, pain, and anger into the here and now. Suddenly I feel that old sense of helplessness and hopelessness wash over me.

The good news is that the slush fund of grief, anger, terror, and pain is diminishing along with the intensity of the overreactions. Of course, when I do overreact, it can startle the other person, as well.

Earlier in life, when I was in the midst of a full-blown panic attack—and they showed up like clockwork—it felt like an elephant was sitting on my chest.

Or it was like someone was inside my chest with a big boot shoving against my ribs. Or like a truck tire was pushing on my chest so it was unable to expand. In the middle of all those panic attacks, I didn't think I would ever, ever be able to verbalize what it felt like. I still can't verbalize it except to say I thought I was losing my mind. I was terrified. Petrified!

Before therapy, I had no idea what was going on. Absolutely no idea! I just knew I needed to get away. I had to get away. But how to get away? Where to go? Sometimes the terror  would be so overwhelming that I'd just take off running into the woods. Once I jumped into my car, drove down an old dirt road, and slept in the vehicle. I had been unable to get away in childhood. Was my brain trying to show me I could get away now? By my own choice?

At some level during my childhood, I perceived somehow that I was being *groomed* to take my mother's place in orchestrating the ritual events, maybe even to become a breeder. I assumed that's why I was never *injured* as badly as some of the other girls were injured or at least appeared to be injured. My mind told me there was no way, no how, that I would ever take my mother's place.

I recall that during one ritual event someone in the circle actually took my hand, placed a knife in it, and raised it above one of the girls who was lying in the center of the circle on a raised platform. My brain knew that I was expected to plunge the knife into her chest. My heart and my hand rebelled against doing that.

In one therapy session, as I related this to the therapists, I cried and cried and cried believing that perhaps I had actually killed the girl. But then my denial kicked in, I guess. I would prefer to believe that the group members orchestrated something to make me think I had actually killed a human being rather than believing I had actually done so. I had similar experiences with my pets. Making me believe I had done something dreadful may have been one technique the adults used to keep me in line.

According to Rita Carter in her book *Mapping the Mind,* attention is very narrowly focused during trauma. Whatever is the center of attention (relevant or incidental) is filed as a sharp flashbulb memory. If trauma is exceptionally severe or prolonged, the stress hormones produced may damage the hippocampus, resulting in a fragmented or incomplete conscious memory. Therapy helped me get some of those memories into consciousness. Some memories came back through my drawings.

Therapy helped me get those memories into conscious awareness. Some memories came back through my drawings. The nightmares and flashbacks are brutal and debilitating, especially those basement memories. As I  mentioned before, I was to stay out of the basement unless I went down there with my parents. I lived in constant fear that if I did something my parents didn't like they might take me to the basement—a fate unto death. Whenever I was taken to the basement something bad happened. Basement trips were always (repeat ALWAYS) associated with some type of pain, sadness, fear, terror, or loss.

Somehow I knew, although nothing had been verbalized specifically, that very bad things would happen to me if I disobeyed. My mother told me over and over again, "Do what you are told to do. Just do what they want you to do." I truly believed that if I did not do exactly as I was instructed something or someone would die—an impossible load for any child to bear.

And always, over and above everything, was the family mantra.

Our secret. Our secret.
Don't tell. Don't tell.

I can't be sure when the really dysfunctional behaviors actually began. Memories of being sexually abused by my parents go back very far. Recollections of the ritual activities go back to at least the age of two. Both types of abuse (sexual and ritual) continued until I was about age ten. Then, suddenly the sexual abuse by my father stopped. It ceased shortly after my being abused by the school janitor, when my father apparently *crossed the line* between what happened during ritual activities and what had happened in real everyday life. At least that's my guess.

For whatever reason, my required attendance at rituals stopped not long after that, as well. I've always wondered about the reason for this. What would cause my parents to stop forcing me to be involved in the rituals? Maybe they really were afraid I'd start remembering what had happened and tell someone.

Childhood sexual abuse is terrifying, but there is also often an element of sexual arousal and longed-for attention in it. The psychology of a child's response to childhood sexual abuse is an extension of normal psychology.

—Colin A. Ross, MD

Silent Screams—
Can No One Hear Me?

Chapter Ten—
Batter Up!

*Until you value yourself, you won't
value your time. Until you value your
time, you will not do anything with it.*

—M. Scott Peck

 My father loved sports, and somehow I inherited that love. He had played softball during his youth, although I never realized that until I was older. I wish I knew more about his history: what team he played with, where he played, and so on. It's a loss that we never really talked about any of his sports' history.

Once in a while my father would play catch with me. But he could be mean and vindictive. I recall playing catch with him when I was about nine. He would throw the ball very hard to see what I would do.

If I threw it back hard, he would get mad and then throw another one to make me scramble or dive. I was only nine years old for heaven's sake! Once, when I threw the ball back the way he had thrown it to me, he stuck his foot out to stop the ball and broke his ankle, ending up with crutches and a cast on his foot. Silence reprised. He became very angry and didn't speak to me for what seemed ages.

My father did, however, expose me to a variety of different sports, one thing for which I'm grateful. Even though I appreciated that, there was little if any follow-up in terms of training. As a teenager I remember being told I could have been a really good bowler and golfer if I had had some coaching. There never was any coaching, never any follow through training.

 When I was age seven, we lived out in the country (again on the edge of a ravine). One day I was using my father's putter to hit golf balls in the front yard, which was probably close to an acre in size. The golf club was nearly as long as I was tall.

My father came outside and kept wanting to give me a iron club, but I kept going back to the putter because I could "hit the ball" with it. It was while he was watching me use the putter that he realized I was hitting the ball on the "wrong side" of the putter.

We finally put two and two together. I am left handed! Especially whenever it comes to activities requiring the use of two hands. Maybe that's why I couldn't do lacrosse very well. Actually, I was pathetic at lacrosse. You need your throwing hand at the top of the stick, which would have been my right hand, but I was totally uncoordinated and hopeless if I tried to use it the way I normally held a two-handed implement.

I am at least ambidextrous but more likely left handed, just having been taught to do activities such as writing and eating with my non-dominant hand.

Twice I recall my father taking me to a driving range, once when I was seven and again when I was ten. Both times the golf pro commented to my father that I was a "natural" and should take lessons. There was always money for booze but never any money available to me for lessons or for green fees. I loved golf, however, and wanted to play so I would collect pop bottles and turn them in for two cents each. I saved the money for green fees and practiced whenever I could.

Some years later I actually won an amateur open women's regional golf tournament.

What fun!

In retrospect, my father would "start" me on a sport and then leave me to flounder. Maybe he forgot about it in his drunken haze; or maybe he just couldn't be bothered. Perhaps he didn't think I was worth his time, or he didn't know how to parent or coach because of the inconsistent experiences he'd had with his absentee alcoholic father.

It might have been all or none of those. Whatever the reason, I regret never having been given the opportunity to really train or be coached in a specific sport. I'm sure I could have been very successful.

Nevertheless, regardless of my parents' lack of follow through, I loved sports. During both high school and university I became quite competent at several. For example, I played softball at a national level. Our team won many awards. I also remember being so excited once when my father showed up to a game. But then I also recall being totally embarrassed because he got very drunk.

 My parents both bowled regularly. I started ten-pin bowling in a league when I was age ten; my father even bought me my own ball when I turned twelve. I was good at bowling and came to love the sport.

Those bowling-league experiences are one of the very few things I recall when the three of us actually did something together as a "family" that seemed somewhat "normal."

My biggest bowling thrill was the year I got to bowl with my parents at a Christmas function. Initially I recall there being some objection to having a 'kid' present. I was the only child there. However, I bowled well—especially well on this occasion, as it turned out. I won the prize: a twenty-pound Christmas turkey!

All the adults were mad.
On the other hand, I remember being really proud to bring that holiday bird home. Even more so when my mother fixed it for dinner!

Although lacking a coach, I did have a few lessons: swimming. For a while when I was about five years old, my father would take me every Saturday morning to a pool that seemed like a long drive to a little kid. The pool too, seemed long and huge. I do remember the feeling of pure joy when I was able to jump into the deep end and dog paddle to the side. On the way home my father would always stop at a little strip mall and buy me a chocolate éclair filled with whipped cream. I don't recall much conversation, but I know that was a special time for us to be together.

In retrospect, however, I've often wondered if he was getting me out of the way because my mother was orchestrating some ritual event. My gut says that's what was happening although I certainly can't prove it.

In spite of receiving little or no encouragement and no coaching, I kept gravitating toward sports. I became involved with one type of sports activity after another. My brain and body seemed to instinctively know how to make the motions and moves required by almost every sport I tried—and I tried a great many:

- bowling
- golf
- softball
- ice hockey
- curling
- fencing
- canoeing
- kayaking
- basketball
- broomball
- volleyball
- rock repelling
- archery
- badminton
- racquetball
- squash
- field hockey (we even got to play a team from Ireland)

And the list goes on. In almost every sport I played, I managed to place (if not win) in competition.

More recently when I competed in some regional adult games, I won a medal in track. Ah, those genetics and epigenetics from my father. Of all the sports, softball was my hands-down favorite. How I loved that game! And I was good at it, becoming known for both hitting and throwing. Again I won at all levels of competition, including nationals.

In fact, a newspaper clipping in my scrapbook has this headline:

AMELIA AT BAT MEANS RUNS!

Both my parents bragged to others about my sport successes but they never ever acknowledged any pride in my accomplishments to me directly, much less  praised me. I cannot recall any affirmations during childhood. In fact, the opposite was true. Whenever my father was unhappy with me (which seemed most of the time) and was willing to do more than just grunt, he tended to say something like: "You should have been twins because you're so _____ _____ _____ _____!"

The fill-in-the-blank words were always negative. Always. The lack of affirmation was accompanied by a lack of practical and vital information. I never received any information about the facts of life (although I'd already received a great deal of inappropriate information through practical experiences with both sexual and ritual abuse).

I picked up far more from kids at school than from anything I ever learned at home. I found out about flossing my teeth only after I enrolled at university. (Sad fact!) It was as though my parents were oblivious to me as a person except for my being a parental sex object and/or being groomed for ritual participation.

Whenever I did hear people, family, or friends talking about me, I never recall hearing anything positive being said, except that I could sit quietly for long periods of time. I know now that this total lack of affirmation impacted every facet of my life, especially in the area of self-worth.

My childhood experiences of pain and terror coupled with a lack of affirmation led me to believe I was worthless as a child, as a human being. And really, if I had been worth something, wouldn't they have protected me?

Wouldn't they have affirmed and validated me? I came to the conclusion that there must be something very wrong with me. Most kids would. I mean, what else could I conclude? If I was okay as a person, if there was nothing wrong with me, my parents wouldn't treat me the way they did, right?

Years later, a comment by author Cheri Huber in her book with June Shiver entitled *There Is Nothing Wrong with You* helped me put this into perspective. Huber wrote:

> *"...Why did they do that to me? Because it was done to them. Because we do what we've been taught..."*

Eventually this helped me feel somewhat sorry for my parents; actually pity them. What they did to me must have been done to them. How very, very sad!

Unfortunately, the perception of worthlessness followed me into adulthood. Even now when people compliment or affirm me, they often say I appear surprised, even stunned. Sometimes, I guess I am.

Who, me?

But I am learning to appreciate—even relish—those positive comments.

Maybe someday I will overcome my astonishment altogether.

The good news is that I am learning how to hone my global self-esteem. I can now appreciate more than just aspects of my specific self-esteem. I have actually begun to value who I am as a person. Getting in touch with my spiritual core and a higher power has enhanced this process. As you may imagine, this new perspective has changed my life.

After all, I now realize that I am the only person who will be with me for my entire life. No one else will ever know me as well as I know myself.

As Dr. Wayne W. Dyer put it:

> *"You cannot be lonely if you like the person you're alone with."*

I like the person I am with.

Me.

And it's ok.

And I'm ok.

Actually I'm better than ok!

Tell me how a person judges his or her self-esteem and I will tell you how that person operates at work, in love, in sex, in parenting, in every important aspect of existence—and how high he or she is likely to rise. The reputation you have with yourself—your self-esteem—is the single most important factor for a fulfilling life. Of all the judgments a person may pass in life, none is more important than the judgment a person passes on the self.

—Nathaniel Branden
How to Raise Your Self-Esteem

I hope I'll Be
Safe In Here...

Chapter Eleven—
Gift of Gratitude

Reflect on your present blessings, of which everyone has many, not on your past misfortunes, of which all have some.

—Charles Dickens

 I have struggled with aspects of negative thinking my entire life.

Still do.

It probably reflects living with so much negativity during childhood. My first thought about almost anything is usually negative. It's as if my brain immediately jumps to the fifteenth hurdle instead of taking them one at a time.

Often the negative thinking ends up with my mind perceiving some picture of violence, devastation, or pain. Hopeless and helpless.

I may find a pair of gloves on one of the woodland trails, and the next thing I know my brain fantasizes about finding a body somewhere. Or I might see a tree down and immediately think: What if it had fallen on me? Who would find me? How would I get help? Or if I happen to twist the wrong way, suddenly my thoughts have me slumped on the floor with dislocations, broken bones, and anxious about not being found for days or weeks—or never.

I believe my sense of helplessness in adulthood, following in the wake of my sense of helplessness in childhood, has contributed to my staying in jobs, relationships, or environments when it would have been much healthier and more functional to leave and move on. But at the time, I was unequipped, uninformed, and powerless to do so.

Along with negativity, there are often pieces (make that chunks) of anger. I now know that anger was the appropriate emotion for many of my childhood experiences. Anger is the emotion that arises to alert a person that his or her boundaries are being invaded. Wow! My boundaries were continually being invaded or I was living in fear that they were about to be invaded yet again. Nevertheless, there is a price to pay for that unresolved anger. These days it bubbles up less and less for me. Given the right circumstances or a powerful enough trigger, however, and there anger is again.

Wham!

Bam!

The "twins:" negative thinking and anger.

Both negative thinking and anger plague me, arising SO fast from somewhere deep in my subconscious. I continually have to take intentional charge of my thoughts and try to change negatives into positives. Even when there is an actual negative event, I can acknowledge it and still choose to look for the lesson, to find the silver lining. Typically something positive does exist, if I look for it.

Along the same lines, I continually have to ask myself if a specific relationship or situation or job or whatever, is good for me. Is it helping me in my recovery or is it reminding my brain of past negative experiences? I have to ask whether or not I need to distance myself from it. I now know that I am no longer helpless and hopeless, but those learned belief systems can be challenging to change.

I also now realize that my ex-husband was a catalyst for my realizing how much anger was bottled up inside. It couldn't have been much fun for him, either, his trying to deal with the fears and ranting and raging that poured out of me in our marriage.

I had never before yelled or been abusive toward another human being in any way, shape, or form. Needless to say those behaviors caught me off guard. I could neither grasp nor explain what was happening. Was I losing my mind?

However, I now realize that this marked the beginning of my body refusing to keep the memories bottled up, the start of my voice refusing to remain mute any longer. The silence itself was starting to fracture. Other triggers emerged. If we were in bed together and he would snuggle up behind me, or even come up behind me in the house, I would become panic-stricken and overreact.

I now realize that those situations simply reminded my subconscious of the ritual abuse, when men in the circle would come up behind me and place their erect member between my poor little buttocks. But in my marriage, I would just experience unexplained panic and terror.

My husband said that I reminded him of a cornered animal, shaking in abject terror. Terror of what? We didn't know. Because of that we started going for couple's therapy, but it was always little more than a Band-Aid. Conversations centered on dealing with my temper, my explosions, and my terror.

Once during a therapy session when the counselor was trying to figure out the origin of my rage, I jumped to my feet and stormed out. Returning a little while later I asked, "Do you think this is going to take a long time?" After all, I was in a hurry. I wanted this to be over and done with.

To my complete and utter dismay the counselor replied, "Yes, I think it will." Dismay was putting it mildly! Now I realize she might have guessed at some of my history, although we hadn't so much as scratched the surface, much less dug down into the basement. I, on the other hand, wasn't even close to looking at that. It was far too terrifying. The brain only gives you as much as you can handle at one time—and that's only if you are willing to remember.

How did others guess at my history before I was able to own it?

My therapists had a pretty good idea of what I would reveal. Several told me later they were fairly certain my anger stemmed from some type of severe sexual abuse.

As Hillary Clinton wrote: *It Takes a Village.* Well, there is no doubt in my mind that I am the recovering, successful survivor that I am today because of *my village*. (Thank you.)

When my therapists recommended books, I became a book worm, reading voraciously. I read about the price of sexual abuse; about the high cost of ritual abuse. I read about self-esteem, attachment or the lack thereof, boundary development and boundary violations, about codependency and grief recovery.

I began to catch a glimpse of the difference between my sense of spirituality and a choice of whether or not to identify with established religion.

Gradually I began to get in touch with my own spiritual part and start to experience a sense of awe again, especially out in nature. I felt safer outside, as I had during childhood. In nature I sensed being part of a bigger picture—of the whole universe. With that, I began to hope that a healthier future was possible. And this sense of hope eventually turned into belief.

I devoured *The Life Recovery Bible* and took a new look at my learned patterns of negative thinking, pessimism, and depression. I wrote a quote by Soren Kierkegaard on the fly leaf and it became one of my goals:

Now with God's help,
I shall become myself.

I read with new understanding advice from the Apostle Paul when he admonished to think about whatever is true, honorable, just, pure, lovely, and gracious. Incorporating this advice into my life, little by little, helped shift my negative trend of thought. As I do that, my thinking style is becoming more positive.

It will be a life-long journey, this struggle to alter the negative thinking patterns ingrained in my brain since early childhood. My sense of hopelessness and helplessness has eased, however. And as my sense of hopelessness and helplessness has eased, so has the anger. It tends to surface much more appropriately, no longer living as an underlying seething mass in my subconscious. Everything is becoming more connected.

As McGinnis described it in his book *The Power of Optimism*, real optimism entails learning how to face all of life's experiences. Healthy, realistic optimism does not search for ways to interpret every event as positive, but realistically confronts and tackles the negative with confidence and hope.

And Peter McWilliams was on the money when he titled his book: *You Can't Afford the Luxury of a Negative Thought.*

I know I cannot!

Gradually I came to believe: "I can do this. I really am able to do this!"

Actually, "I *am* doing this!"

According to Dr. Candace Pert, author of *Molecules of Emotion*, memories are stored not only in the brain but also at the cellular receptor level throughout the psychosomatic network. Memory processes are emotion-driven and unconscious. Unconscious memories, once formed, impact a person's in-the-moment perception. In turn, this impacts both body biochemistry and hormone production.

With clear intent and the implementation of appropriate strategies, at least some of these memories may be brought to conscious awareness. Awareness is always the first step. You can only deal effectively with what you can become aware of, label, and describe.

I am more aware of my thoughts and course-correct, taking immediate action as needed, and looking for the humor. If I perceive that humor isn't appropriate in the given situation, I move into gratitude.

In fact, I think of it as a formula:

Awareness plus Humor and Gratitude equal Better Health.

According Doc Childre and Howard Martin, authors of *The HeartMath Solution*, positive emotions such as happiness, compassion, love, and appreciation tend to increase the level of order and balance in the nervous system. Developing a positive mindset and choosing to dwell on positive emotions and thoughts, not only reduce the production of the stress hormone cortisol but also create harmonious heart rhythms.

I am definitely honing the skill of gratitude. The good news is that it is physiologically impossible to be fearful and appreciative at the same time. Choosing to be grateful for something, anything, even in the face of fear, helps my brain feel safer. Gratitude has helped me avoid unnecessary downshifting and enabled me to upshift more quickly, as needed.

These strategies help to reduce the impact of stressors, enable me to perceive the world more clearly, and benefit not only my brain but also my heart, body, and immune system.

Gratitude unlocks the fullness of life.
It turns what we have into enough, and
more... Gratitude makes sense of our
past, brings peace for today, and
creates a vision for tomorrow.

—Melody Beattie

I Must Be Hypervigilant—
I Hold
the Key To My Heart

Chapter Twelve—
Double Jeopardy

Life shrinks or expands in proportion to one's courage.

—Anaïs Nin

 I saw little evidence of affection or positive emotions between my parents. Very little. So I remember vividly one time when my dad was standing in the kitchen getting a beer and my mom walked by him and gave him a semi hug across his tummy. They always kissed each other at Christmas when they got a present.

Chastely.

Other than that, affection wasn't very apparent. I never knew until I visited some of my friends' homes later that people actually "said" they loved each other and "touched" one another affectionately. What a concept!

I recall one long period of silence (a five-week stretch, I think) during which my father never spoke to me even once. That was a record. My mother had gone away to attend a Shriners' convention. Prior to her departure, he would grunt at my mom, but whenever I would come into the room, he would walk out. So I presume that he was ticked off at me for something. I was probably about eighteen then, attending a local college. During that agonizing time I just avoided him and kept myself busy and engaged in my college studies and my sports.

One evening I returned home after a long day and a great basketball game. Hungry, I decided to make myself a dinner to celebrate. I grilled a T-bone steak with barbeque sauce that my mother had left. I cooked corn on the cob, and sliced a beef steak tomato that was nearly three inches in diameter, salivating the whole time I was getting things ready.

I sat my plate on the kitchen counter, getting ready to take it into the dining room table. As I turned to get some salt and dill for the tomato slices, my father walked into the kitchen. (I can still feel the knot in my chest and *see* him in my mind's eye entering the room.) He was between me and the counter. I thought to myself: *Now what? Do I leave? Do I grab my food and eat in my room? What should I do? What will happen?*

He was still dressed from work. Tie off, top button of his white shirt undone, with crisp starched cuffs and collar. Picking up *my* plate, he mumbled, "Is this mine? Thanks." And just like that he consumed *my* dinner as if I had prepared it caringly for HIM. I was both furious and relieved. Furious, because he took my special dinner. (Cooking is not something I typically enjoy doing). Relieved, because I knew that the weeks of silence were over, for the time being. There would be similar episodes of silence in the future.

I just took the leftovers and made myself a sandwich.

Shortly after that incident my parents informed me they were moving. This would put us on opposite coasts of the country unless I wanted to move with them. Much later I discovered the reason for their move. It had been necessitated because my father had had a rather messy affair with one of the secretaries in his office. (Those *wandering hands* again!)

Incidentally, that was also the first time I ever heard my parents argue. Listening against the wall in the bathroom, glass to my ear, I heard my mother's side of a conversation with my father over the phone. It was very obvious what they were talking about. That was the first time I'd ever heard my mother raise her voice.

I heard her say, "Amelia doesn't need to know anything about this."

More silence.

I elected to remain and attend university with my friends and team mates. My parents gave me a week to find a place to live. I managed to rent a basement suite in a private home just before they were due to leave.

I'm not sure I'd want my 18-year-old daughter 3,000 miles away on her own, but they didn't seem to have any problem with it. I found a part time job and worked my way all through school. My parents sent me a little money once in a while and occasionally I'd receive a package from my mom containing food. They each wrote me separate letters and that told me they weren't talking to one another during much of this time.

When I finished a Bachelor's degree in teaching and secondary education, my parents flew out to attend my graduation. They were proud—not of me but for them. This was *their daughter!* And the first in the entire family to earn a degree! They attended an evening baccalaureate function, as well as the actual march and graduation. After the ceremony they came back to my place and invited *their* friends over for a small tea. None of my friends were invited.

During the tea, my folks passed around the graduation card they had brought so everyone could see it. When it got to me, I glanced inside, saw what I thought was a two dollar bill, and was a little ho-hum about it.

"Did you look inside the card?" my mother asked.

"Yes," I replied. "It's a two dollar bill."

But when I doubled checked, I discovered that it was, in fact, a $1,000 dollar bill! Both bills were similar in color and I assumed they had given me two dollars. Not only embarrassed, I again felt *on display* for their benefit in front of their friends. Again I felt like I was somehow being *bought* with their generosity, much as with the excessive display of Christmas gifts. I would have liked to just hear them say just once how happy they were for me, that they knew how hard I had worked. They never did. I know I was relieved when they returned home.

At age 24 I married for the first time. Less than a year later I discovered that my husband was having an affair with one of my friends, signaling the beginning of the end for that relationship. I recall thinking that our baggage matched, my husband's and mine. I had a father who had affairs; I married a man who had affairs.

My second marriage was to a man who exhibited behaviors that typically correlate with sexual abuse in childhood. Talk about double jeopardy! As with my first marriage, that meant that our baggage matched: sexual dysfunction and emotional unavailability. At the time I certainly did not realize (as Dana Crowley Jack put it), that when low self-esteem prevents a woman from believing she will be loved for free, for her own qualities and characteristics, she chooses a damaged partner she intends to help.

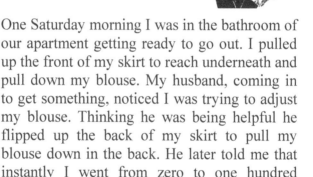

One Saturday morning I was in the bathroom of our apartment getting ready to go out. I pulled up the front of my skirt to reach underneath and pull down my blouse. My husband, coming in to get something, noticed I was trying to adjust my blouse. Thinking he was being helpful he flipped up the back of my skirt to pull my blouse down in the back. He later told me that instantly I went from zero to one hundred percent ballistic.

"What do you think you are doing?" I screamed. "Don't ever, *ever* do that again!"

Of course neither one of us had any idea where in the wide-wide world that explosion came from nor what it meant. It did start us down the path to arguing. We argued regularly.

We argued about nothing.

We argued about everything.

We argued about arguing.

From the perspective of today, I'm so very grateful for that trigger event in the bathroom, although it precipitated a terrible time of argument. I realize it was the catalyst that began my unraveling, which later helped me make sense of my life.

As we went from argument to argument, as one argument ran into another, I'd find myself crying several times a day. I spiraled down into profound depression accompanied by debilitating fatigue. When I didn't have to show up at work, I'd wake up in the morning and think about breakfast, fall back asleep until noon, and then wonder where the time went.

I began having panic attacks but couldn't identify any reason. I didn't even recognize what they were at that point. I just knew that I was on high alert for "something" and typically would respond inappropriately.

On work days, I dragged myself to the office, often more zombie than not. One morning a colleague asked, "What were you doing in grade four, Amelia?"

Almost immediately I could name all my teachers, all my schools, all my houses, everything—except for the year when I was nine. Those memories were missing. The fact that I couldn't recall that year started to worry me. I became anxious and began to obsess with remembering. In the process I became even more depressed and angry.

Then one day I had a flashback. It was a brief but very clear picture of the day in fourth grade when the school janitor pulled me into his janitor closet and molested me. Crying, I had run home and told my father about the incident, whereupon he had become angry and sexually abused me on the living room floor saying "You are for me. Me!"

When my mother walked in to the room and saw my father sexually abusing me in the *conscious* world, she went ballistic. Until then, my parents had kept the real world and the ritual world completely separate and apart. Evidently, molesting his daughter outside the safety of a ritual activity crossed some line.

 After that incident, I was taken back to the ravine and the terror escalated. Something had changed, however, as I was never again taken down to the basement.

After I recalled the incident with the school janitor, other incidents came flooding into conscious memory. I became physically ill and eventually sought the help of a skilled therapist. The memories terrified me, especially as more and more surfaced during therapy.

Slowly but surely I began to identify my pent-up rage. Slowly but surely I began to understand the reasons for my violent overreaction when my husband had pulled up the back of my skirt. It had reminded my brain of the many times in the basement and in the ravine when men in the ritual group had sexually assaulted me, urinated on me, and then walked away.

I recalled overhearing a conversation about my beloved cocker spaniel, Preemie (so named because she actually had been born prematurely). One day, while visiting the neighbors, a family also involved in my parents' ritual group, I chanced to hear them talking about Preemie. I remembered running home sobbing and begging my mother not to let Preemie be killed. It didn't help. My beloved Preemie was dismembered anyway, right in front of me, the first of several. My body was releasing memories it could no longer keep buried.

Once the dam cracked, it soon broke wide open. Memories from the year I was nine flooded into consciousness. It was during that year when one of my girlfriends was killed during a ritual gathering. At least I have a very strong sense that she died but they could have just made it look like she died. Those who orchestrate rituals are often very good at using "smoke and mirrors" tactics to keep their victims horrified and under their control. I am not sure, but it definitely felt like she did die. Certainly I never saw her again.

So those two traumatic events, the "deaths" of my dog and my girlfriend, undoubtedly were part of the reason the entire year was missing from my memory. And all of those hidden-away memories were brought to my brain's consciousness awareness by my colleague's innocent question: "What were you doing in grade four, Amelia?"

Thanks to my seasoned, talented, and patiently persistent therapists, I began to not only come to grips with the memories in my mind but also with the memories in my body. I learned to recognize and differentiate the parts of my body that were almost frozen stiff with terror and sadness while other parts were so tender I could hardly bear to have them touched.

My mind may have forgotten; my body—never.

I did a week-long intensive in Somatherapy that surfaced additional memories, releasing stored painful energy. The process was grueling and excruciating as my body *relived* the stored trauma. It also triggered the healing process in ways too numerous to recount. Yes, it was brutal, but the positive outcome was that, for the first time in years, I could actually touch parts of my own body (e.g., ears, eyebrows, and throat) without experiencing intense pain.

> Somatherapy (or Soma) exercises work with the relationship between the body and the emotions.

In one session I recall crying and screaming as one scene after another flashed in front of my eyes. There was everything from my grandfather forcing me to watch brutality being heaped on another child or animal to him finally pulling me up by my one arm out of a deep excavation pit. I knew I wasn't going to die after all—not on that day, at least. But I carried pain in that shoulder for years.

My therapists recognized and helped me identify the terror and sadness I had lived with for decades. They helped me identify it for what it was. Pure evil.

What an oxymoron! Pure. Evil.

The day during therapy when I recalled my father flipping me onto my stomach and sexually assaulting me from behind when I was just a little girl, with my mother watching as I lay there in abject and excruciating pain, I suddenly understood the blouse episode. The body always remembers. It knows what it knows. It cannot forget the pain. It cannot forget the deprivation. When there is deprivation at that level, there is a huge hole that is always there, waiting to be filled.

As I recalled more and more episodes of terror and abuse, my therapists helped me acknowledge and accept how much my mother, father, grandfather, and many others had hurt me in every way imaginable.

And on the day in therapy when I could finally own all that knowledge, my body began to shake; to shake uncontrollably. My teeth chattered and clattered and all I could do was moan: "They really hurt me, they really hurt me."

And they had really hurt me.

Hurt me badly!

In her book *The Body Never Lies,* Alice Miller writes:

> *Experience has taught me that my own body is the source of all the vital information that has enabled me to attain greater autonomy and self-confidence. Only when I allowed myself to feel the emotions pent up for so long inside me did I start extricating myself from my own past.*

She was right.

When the pain became more than I could tolerate, my therapists would often watch me dissociate, see my mind drift off somewhere where it wouldn't hurt so much. I know now that I used to do that when my father and grandfather would kick me from behind or do other things to me from behind.

When I would dissociate, my therapists would bring me back to reality and help me understand that although I couldn't protect myself back then, I could take care of myself now; that the things that had been done to me during childhood need never happen again.

Ever.

Often they told me I was very brave, that I had immense courage.

I couldn't really "get" that at first because I'd not been able to protect myself during childhood. As I began to recover and heal, however, I came to understand I had done the best I could in childhood.

I had survived.

That helped me to take a look at learned helplessness and make more empowering choices in my life. I am very clear now on personal boundaries and take good care of myself.

I am reparenting myself.

I am no longer helpless.

I am no longer hopeless.

From the time of late gestation and birth, we begin to develop a template of expectations about ourselves and other people, anticipating responsiveness or indifferences, success or failure. This is when the foundation of who we become and how we relate to others and to the world around us is built. Neurobiology conforms to the environment so that the young brain quickly reflects the cumulative impact of child-parent interactions.

—Robin Karr-Morse, Meredith S. Wiley
Ghosts from the Nursery

This Is No Way
To Exist—
Live Or Die, I MUST
Find My Voice...

Chapter Thirteen— Getting on Board

When we speak we are afraid our words will not be heard or welcomed. But when we are silent, we are still afraid. So it is better to speak.

—Audre Lorde

"This is Amelia Baker," I said into the phone.

"Amelia! How are you?" came the immediate reply.

"I'm in therapy," I said, hesitantly.

"Good for you," she said. "I'm glad."

I waited a minute, half thinking I might hear something like: *What took you so long?* or *It's about time!* or *Better late than never.* She just asked again, "How are you, Amelia?" Right, I hadn't answered her question.

"I'm doing much better," I said, taking a deep breath and pausing a moment. "You were right. I *am* angry. *Very angry.* About a lot of things. Mostly from childhood. I was angry when we had our four-hour conversation years ago. I've probably been angry my entire life. I just didn't know it."

Again I expected her to say something like *"Duh!"* Instead she laughed and said, "You may recall I got up to 'stretch my legs' several times during that conversation. I was really moving my nose out of striking range from your fist, just in case your rage got out of hand."

"Was it really that obvious?" I asked.

"It was to me," she replied. "And I'm proud of you, Amelia. It's not always easy to recognize and admit something like that, much less do the work required to uncover the source."

Proud of me? *She* was *proud* of *me*?

For the life of me I couldn't recall either my parents or grandparents ever saying they were proud of me. Oh sure, they'd been proud of my sport's ability and successes, bragging about those to their friends. But they had never told me they were proud of *me* and certainly never for just being *me*, Amelia. Wow! This was so special to hear.

"Feel free to keep me posted on your progress, should you choose to do so," she said. "Share whatever you want, as little or as much as is comfortable for you. I'll be interested. Just remember, I'm a brain-function specialist and neither a therapist nor an abuse counselor."

We hung up. As I put down the phone, I froze momentarily. She'd said *abuse counselor!* How did she know we were talking about *abuse?* Yikes!

Several months later the mail brought a card announcing another brain-program weekend. I was becoming increasingly interested in brain function and this would be another opportunity for us to connect in person. I decided to attend.

The information presented was amazing. I learned so much about myself! Some things I already knew in a vague way, but now they were being validated. My sensory preference is kinesthetic, which means that sensory stimuli related to touch, taste, smell, temperature perception, and muscle coordination register most quickly and intensely in my brain.

That was an Ah-ha that helped explain why I may have experienced more discomfort and pain from my early childhood experiences than a child might have who had an auditory or visual preference.

I thought a lot about that. After all, the skin is the largest body organ. And I am still SO particular about what I wear. All my clothing, must—MUST—feel comfortable against my skin, with nothing tight or scratchy. No wonder there were parts of my body that hurt terribly or that I could not bear to have touched. Any child abused as I had been would likely have tender body sites. But for a kinesthetic, it was huge.

Discovering that piece of information made me feel more "normal" and less like this weirdo who was so unbelievably sensitive to whatever touched her. It also helped explain some of my sports giftedness. I had an exceptionally fine use of my musculature and could learn and perform sports-related activities often more quickly and competently than others. It was affirming to understand about "me."

I developed a better understanding of the consequences of chronic stress. I love it when things start making sense, and this insight was so validating. When the body becomes stressed and activates a stress response, all senses become heightened. If stress is chronic, the senses are constantly on red alert and sensory burnout can result. Eventually, the decoding of all sensory data can become less efficient over time.

I had experienced such sensory changes, including convoluted sight, limited taste sensations, and neuropathy on the skin of my head, shoulders, and back. I also suffered from a reduced ability to judge water temperature in the kitchen, shower, and bathtub, which required constant vigilance on my part to avoid getting burned. That got me wondering about my parents' sensory preferences. With all my mother's skin-touching and interest in food and cooking, it's possible she was kinesthetic, too. She did love to eat and both she and her mother had been quite overweight.

My father, on the other hand, used so little verbal language that he probably wasn't auditory. Maybe visual. He always looked quite nice when he dressed up for work. And yet he'd been good at sports, too, so maybe kinesthetic? It was fun to conjecture.

I also found it helpful to identify my natural "right-brained" abilities, finally owning that I had innate giftedness in areas that allowed me to be creative, especially in the arts. Before my arthritis interfered, I had thoroughly enjoyed working in stained glass. Now it made sense how I could whistle all around a melody, adding embellishments here and there, very improvisational.

During adolescence I had been labeled a tomboy (perhaps one in ten girls are). That, too, made sense. The types of sports at which I had excelled used the large-muscle groupings of the body, which align more with frontal-lobe brain function (the posterior lobes of the cerebrum favoring smaller muscle and eye-hand movements).

And, yes, I probably am innately left-handed, with my ambidexterity likely a result of growing up in a right-handed world. Because I am definitely left handed doing two handed activities (e.g., golf club, bat, broom), I explored practicing one-handed activities, such as eating and writing, with my left hand. Granted, I'd have to learn some new skills, but if I were genuinely meant to be left-handed, living that way could require less energy expenditure for my brain.

One evening during the seminar, the speaker and I were able to eat dinner together, just the two of us. We sat a little apart from the other tables, conversing in low tones. She listened intently as I recounted childhood memories that were bubbling to the surface as a result of my counseling and therapy processes.

Finally, putting down her fork and folding her hands beneath her chin, she looked at me for a long moment.

Then she suggested that I get my memories "out on paper" in front of me. "Just start writing things down," she said. "Whatever you recall whenever you recall it. Maybe, eventually, what you write will turn into a book."

I may have overreacted just a tad. "Are you kidding?" I blurted loudly. Then sensing other people were looking at me, I lowered my voice and whispered, "You can't be serious!" She nodded.

My mind raced. A book? I can't write a book! She doesn't know the half of what happened to me. I can hardly verbalize, let alone put down on paper the pain and terror; the hurt and shivering from multiple betrayals, the false guilt and shame that had been heaped upon me; the isolation and silence; feelings of inadequacy and worthlessness along with the sense that my body was not mine to control; the helplessness and hopelessness. Besides, she doesn't understand how that wouldn't be safe. Break the silence? Expose the secrets? I don't dare talk about what had happened to me in any public way. Some of those people are still alive; quite a few, in fact. Oh, there would be retribution from some quarter if I talked. Definitely there would be retribution.

No! No way is this going to happen!

Immediately my mind slipped into a replay of the old familiar mantra. Around and around went the words:

Our secret. Our secret.
Don't tell. Don't tell.

I surprised myself when I didn't dissociate, but I'm quite sure I downshifted during our conversation. Obviously noticing my agitation, the subject was dropped as we returned to eating.

Of course time passed and I wrote nothing. Not one word. Periodically, as our paths crossed, albeit infrequently, she would bring up the topic again. Gently.

Once she suggested that writing about what happened might help me release some of my fear. Writing might not only be healing for me but also might give hope to others and help other survivors figure out a way to recover and find inner healing; help them believe it was possible to move away from hopelessness and learned helplessness.

I kept shaking my head. I did not want to go through the details again. I'd been through them. More than enough times than I cared to remember and with several different therapists, for heaven's sake!

Been through them until I no longer felt like fainting or panicking from the memories, feeling less guilt and shame, and no longer turning my sense of hopelessness into a hope for death.

A book? Never!

A couple years later our paths crossed again. This time she offered to help me write the book. "Just jot down your recollections as they come to you," she said, the idea being that eventually she'd get them into some type of organization and hire an editor to help turn them into something a bit more formal. "Like chapters in a book."

"It could help you make sense out of the nonsense of your childhood," she said, giving me back some of my own words. Okay, that sounded doable (almost) and not nearly so overwhelming. I could agree with that. My childhood had been one unending saga of nonsense, although I typically thought of it as *non-sense*. "This could help put perspective into the pieces of your journey, help validate in your own mind what you've experienced, chart the progress you've made and are making in recovery, outline where you have been, where you are going, and how you want to spend the rest of your life," she said. "Oh, and it could also help you find your voice."

Help me find my voice? Hmmm. I was now becoming intrigued. I would be so grateful if my story could be told and my voice heard in order to help someone else who might need to be encouraged.

Growing up I had had no *voice*. Oh, I had had a physical voice, but I almost never used it at home and as little as possible at school. In adulthood I used it in my teaching and coaching. But I had never used my voice to speak aloud about my life experiences except to a few trusted individuals—and then at a very superficial level.

Even during therapy sessions my *voice* was much more likely to come out in drawings—in "silent screams" when the therapeutic masseuse would press too hard on a specific spot or get too close to a danger zone.

Help me find my voice? What an empowering thought. I started to feel excitement at the prospect of being heard! The way she threw it out there so casually made it sound possible. Like I could actually write down some of what had happened to me.

MY voice?
Mine?

Then again, no. Whom was I kidding? What would I say? Who would believe my story? I wasn't a writer.

It would be just another exercise in wasted effort, discouragement, hopelessness, pain, and shame. Far better to leave it alone, let sleeping dogs lie. That was the ticket. Let sleeping dogs lie.

"Stop thinking about any of that," she said. "Write it down for me. Let *me* read it."

I could maybe do *that*. Maybe. I was starting to have confidence in her, so I said I'd think about it—partly just to get out of making any commitment and partly because I knew I'd be embarrassed putting my story down on paper. I told her as much.

"Embarrassment is a choice," she replied, calmly. "Avoid going there. You are a survivor. That's far more amazing."

I let that affirmation sink in.

I've since learned that there is a difference between healthy guilt or shame and unhealthy guilt or shame. Healthy guilt and shame remind you that you're human. Humans make mistakes and they can learn from those mistakes. False guilt and shame implies that you yourself are a mistake, you deserve what is being heaped upon you, and there is nothing you can do about it.

Help me find my voice. I am a survivor. I have a story to tell. Those phrases rolled around and around inside my head.

Soon after that seminar, someone sent me a card imprinted with words attributed to Joseph Epstein. They read:

> *We do not choose to be born. We do not choose our parents. We do not choose our historical epoch, or the country of our birth, or the immediate circumstances of our upbringing. We do not, most of us, choose to die; nor do we choose the time or conditions of our death. But within all this realm of choicelessness, we do choose how we shall live: courageously or in cowardice, honorably or dishonorably, with purpose or adrift. We decide what is important and what is trivial in life. We decide that what makes us significant is either what we do or what we refuse to do. But no matter how indifferent the universe may be to our choices and decisions, these choices and decisions are ours to make. We decide. We choose. And as we decide and choose, so are our lives formed. In the end, forming our own destiny is what ambition is about.*

Those words really grabbed my attention and started me thinking about *my story,* about choosing to live courageously, with intention and purpose, about what was really important in my life versus what was trivial. But almost immediately I'd get panic stricken and frightened. Then I'd put the thoughts of writing a book—of giving my story a voice—out of my mind.

More time went by and the idea surfaced and resurfaced. Persisted.

Sometimes, at the thought of being validated and affirmed, I'd become almost breathless. What if readers don't believe me? But this could be just for *me.* Scary thought, that.

More time went by. Once more she offered to find an editor and help me get my story published, if I would just *write,* put my memories down on paper. "It's your voice," she said. "I cannot be your voice. I can help you organize what you write. I can work with an editor on your behalf. However," she continued, "it seems obvious that you don't really want to do this project and I have no agenda for you. So I'll stop offering."

I knew she meant it.

Thoughts and questions raced through my mind. *Do I trust her to help me find my voice? Do I trust her with my story?* Finally, after years of indecision, uncertainty, fear, and hesitancy—the answer was yes. YES!!

I started to write. It wasn't easy, mind you, but it was far less difficult than I had expected. I actually looked forward to each chapter, finding my voice through the writing, hearing my voice on paper.

I selected a working title for my book, too. "It's your story" she said. "You choose." Many title options crossed my mind:

- *Unraveled*
- *Falling Apart and Coming Together*
- *Betrayed*
- *My House of Secrets*
- *My Life—a Circus.*

The word *circus* suggested a spectacle, the unusual, the sensational, or the theatrical. Nothing that would represent real life for most people, yet that certainly fit my childhood. On the other hand, the word *circus* also typically conveys a sense of fun, happiness, anticipation, or pleasure. That certainly *did not* fit.

Finally, I settled on a title: *Beyond the House of Silence.* My house had been a house of silence. Literally. For days and weeks a years at a time. And it had been a house of silence, metaphorically, because of the secrets layered upon secrets. But I was finding my voice and moving beyond *silence.*

I thought about how that title would look on the cover of a book. The cover! I needed a picture for the cover! "It's your story," she said. "You choose."

I knew what I wanted. Years ago I had seen a painting that had completely resonated with me, although I hadn't yet uncovered the reason. It pictured a little girl standing in a corner, obviously in trouble, in disgrace, her faithful little dog beside her—her only friend. I sensed they both were being punished, but for what?

That painting represented something that I and my dog would experience on more than one occasion. Confusion! Fear! Shame! A theme that would run through my life until it became a thread of undoing.

Although I searched and searched, I was unable to find the original painting or a contact who might give me permission to use it on the book cover. Dr. Taylor knew an artist, who agreed to paint a picture based on my description. So now I had a working title and a cover picture.

A pseudonym!

I needed a pseudonym. That much I knew. Again she said, "It's your story. You choose." So I did.

I chose *Amelia Baker.* It felt great; exhilarating! Better than I ever expected it would!

With a title, a pseudonym, and a cover picture, I'm giving the writing of this book my best shot and most sincere effort.

In some ways it feels strange to see my words outside of me, out in front, on paper. It also feels gratifying and empowering. I hope my willingness to do this will prove useful to somebody, to those who perhaps don't believe anything like this really happens to children.

To the skeptics, I would say, "Yes, it does. I'm living proof. And we need to do everything we can to protect them. I choose to use my voice to speak up on their behalf."

To those who have a similar story I would say, "I regret that this happened to you. You have my empathy. I encourage you to do everything you can to find your voice and to move beyond your *house of silence.*"

Take the first step in faith. You don't have to see the whole staircase, just take the first step.

—Dr. Martin Luther King, Jr.

Chapter Fourteen—
Payoff for Persistence

We endure so much more than we think we can, all human experience testifies to that. All we need to do is learn not to be afraid of the pain. Grit your teeth and let it hurt. Don't deny it, don't be overwhelmed by it. It will not last forever. One day the pain will be gone and you'll still be here.

—Harold Kushner

 Kushner was right. I know that now. The pain lessens with every passing day. I'm still here. And with every passing day, life is getting better. Gradually I learned, acknowledged, and finally internalized that I need protection, safety, nurture, affirmation, value, worth, validation, encouragement, trust and care, affection, assurance, security, to be proud of and honor myself, and to be loved.

157

We all need those things. I just never knew that, and I certainly didn't know how to articulate it. Fortunately, my therapists practiced with me and role-played with me, giving me the words to use when I needed or wanted something. Finally, I was on my own path to recovery.

When I got into recovery (because I felt like I was going crazy), I would see my therapist three and four times a week for a couple of hours each time. It was so completely overwhelming, however, that in between sessions I would do nothing but sleep. I remember being continually exhausted.

There was a point where I was suicidal. I knew I didn't want to live any longer with all the pain. But I was too chicken to actually kill myself because at some level I didn't really want to die. I just wanted the pain to stop. I just wanted my body to stop hurting when I told the therapists about what had happened to me. It was such a mixed up time. No wonder my husband left. I would have left me, too, had there been any place I could go! There wasn't.

 No exaggeration, I probably spent upwards of $30,000 in therapy that first year alone. $30,000! That was an obscene amount of money for me, and it completely depleted my savings. However, I am likely alive because of my therapists.

I can laugh about it now (a little), but one day when asked if I was depressed, my response was, "Me? Depressed? No, of course not."

The next question was, "Do you ever cry?"

I said, "Well, yeah."

As we talked, I came to the realization that I'd actually been crying almost every day for over two months. This was startling because I never cried growing up. I was never allowed to show any type of emotion in our house or at rituals. Expressing any type of emotion was unacceptable. In ritual situations, expressing any emotion would just escalate the intensity of whatever was going on at the moment.

After teaching for eight years in high school, I burned out.

Completely.

Having been told what to do my entire childhood, it should have come as no surprise that I gravitated toward a rules-based Christian denomination, one that told me what to do in every particular. Being both proscriptive and conservative, it helped me feel safer at some level because everything was spelled out in detail.

There were no surprises.

In all fairness, I gained substantial numbers of skills and acquired a vast amount of information from my association with that denomination. I taught seminars constantly and honed my speaking skills. I made presentations on stress reduction, grief recovery, boundary development, women's health, and spiritual studies.

It also agreed to take the plunge for a second time and married a man who belonged to the same denomination. Less than two years later he left and moved thousands of miles away. According to him, my erratic behaviors and unexplained rages were the reason.

During that time, my body started saying *NO.* It began to react to the physical and emotional damage that I had experienced and then repressed.

In her book *The Body Never Lies* Alice Miller wrote:

> *Individuals who believe they feel what they ought to feel and constantly do their best not to feel will ultimately fall ill—unless, that is, they leave it to their children to pick up the check by projecting onto them the emotions they cannot admit to themselves.*

Alice Miller hit the nail square on. Ultimately I fell ill and was diagnosed with severe and incapacitating Polymyalgia Rheumatica. I was able to move only with large amounts of pain medication. It took another five years for doctors to reach a more accurate diagnosis of Rheumatoid Arthritis. I was so crippled that I was unable to live alone. It was then that the doctors sent me to a rehabilitation center. Talk about a low point in my life. Talk about scary!

I was so incapacitated by the disease that I was unable to dress or undress or attend to my own toileting. I couldn't brush my own teeth much less my hair or even pick up a drinking cup.

I also developed eye problems: retinal bleeds and macular distortion in my right eye, which required seven different lazer surgeries, a posterior vitrectomy, and one cataract surgery, all side effects from a previous surgery and related medications.

 To say that my active life was negatively impacted would be putting it mildly. Prior to these illnesses, my involvement in sports (like kayaking, hiking, jogging, playing racquet ball, and walking) had helped to compensate for the boiling volcano of repressed emotions with.

The aerobic exercise had helped to dissipate elevated levels of cortisol that my brain and body had released during the decades of chronic stress. Deprived of that type of physical outlet, I spiraled down into depression and existed in a state of sadness and apathy. Much of the time I was probably downshifted, as well.

As my body crumbled into virtual inactivity, my mind rocketed into intense activity. Bit by bit my brain began to give up bits and pieces of repressed memories. I began to draw and paint and construct in pictures what I could not describe in words. Images of abuse that had occurred prior to the development of language flowed out in my drawings. I was frightened by what I saw leaping off the pages.

Just as my subconscious self had become overwhelmed with terror and anxiety and had tried to repress those memories, my conscious self now became overwhelmed with the recollections. In the process of trying to deal with them I realized how truly angry I was. I'd probably been angry for years and years. Furious, actually, and I'd had no clue. Only as my brain aged and could no longer keep the anger bottled up had the rage finally showed. I *was* angry. Very angry.

Truth be told, I was *livid!*

Fetal learning occurs during pregnancy. Once the child is born, learning can proceed very quickly indeed. So can the formation of memories. Although my memories were fragmented, multitudinous, painful, vicious, and almost overwhelming, at last there were recollections to validate a basis for my anger. My brain was able to connect those recollections with all that bottled-up rage.

My body had borne the anger for years. Decades. It had paid the price of that protective emotion. As my mind now began to deal with some of that anger, I felt slightly better, physically. It was a trade-off of sorts. But as my body improved, my brain and nervous system now were exhausted from identifying and dealing with the memories and the rage. And what a vicious cycle.

> *The walls we build around us to keep out the sadness, also keep out the joy.*
>
> —Jim Rohn

In addition to sadness, depression, and grief, I exhibited symptoms of both borderline personality disorder (BPD) and posttraumatic stress disorder (PTSD). Studies have connected both those conditions in adulthood with a history of childhood abuse. I also exhibited symptoms of dissociation, although I was never diagnosed with Dissociative Identity Disorder (DID).

I read Dr. Peter A. Levine's book *Waking the Tiger—Healing Trauma.* Several times, in fact, because it was so helpful. I learned to allow my body to quiver and shake when I would surface a painful memory for the first time. That's part of the body's recovery process and interfering with that process instead of just letting it occur, can actually prevent healing and recovery. The author also points out that people can become victims of their own thoughts, and self-image.

Levine wrote:

> *One of the most profound and conceptually challenging aspects of healing trauma is understanding the role played by memory... Even if we are able to dredge up reasonably accurate memories of an event, they will not heal us.*

I know that to be true. Just recovering a memory in and of itself may not be healing. By just rehearsing the painful memories, a person can actually promote the stress response and become retraumatized. I know that to be true for me. I chose to use the memories to validate reasons for my behavioral symptoms.

With the help of my therapists, I purposed to move onward through the recovery process and create more functional behaviors. Sometimes I felt as if I were moving at the speed of a herd of turtles, sometimes at a snail's pace, but I believed that the process could and would promote long-term healing.

It worked.

In fact, just creating more functional behaviors (even when there were no specific memories that could be recalled) contributed to my recovery and healing process.

Unfortunately, the abuse I experienced resulted in my failure to create appropriate personal limits. And because of those boundary issues, it was decades before I was able to risk even searching for my voice, much less succeed in finding it. And when I finally found it, then I had to choose to use it, had to practice actually using it, rather than just thinking the thoughts inside my head.

In essence, I had to teach myself to speak up. No small feat! At first my voice was just a tiny squeak, metaphorically. Then it became a mere hesitant whisper.

Speak up, Amelia!

Over time it gradually steadied, strengthened, and attained a more normal volume. I believe that I now use my real voice, literally and metaphorically, all the time.

Well, to be honest, most of the time anyway.

And the progress continues!

One of the unique things about the human brain is that it can do only what it thinks it can do. The minute you say, "My memory isn't what it used to be" or "I can't remember a thing today," you are actually training your brain to live up to your diminished expectations. Low expectations mean low results...your brain is always eavesdropping on your thoughts. As it listens, it learns. If you teach it about limitations, your brain will become limited.

—Rudolph E. Tanzi, PhD
Deepak Chopra MD
Super Brain.

From Basement
Terror To Light of
Recovery . . .

Chapter Fifteen—
Steps to Freedom

There is no magic cure, no making it all go away forever. There are only small steps upward; an easier day, an unexpected laugh, a mirror that doesn't matter anymore. I am thawing.

—Laurie Halse Anderson

 As I worked through the discovery and recovery processes, I came to acknowledge that I had been living in a state of extremely high internal stress for as far back as I could remember. Likely well before the age of two. At some level, my brain and body had been continually anxious, fearful, confused, terrified, angry, or in pain.

My therapists were amazing. Knowledgeable. Dedicated. Compassionate. Talented. Patient. Committed. Persistent. Affirming. Validating. Encouraging.

When I started therapy, the first question always was, "Tell me about your family."

And I would answer, "I had a great family, a wonderful childhood, and good experiences. My parents really loved me."

Maybe they did. I can't really second guess that.

But when I think about it now it's like, *Oh really?* My mother and father were both alcoholics and were neglectful, distant, and disaffirming. They both sexually abused me and allowed others to abuse me physically, emotionally, mentally, and sexually. What part of that was "*love?*"

After my father retired, he and my mother moved back across the country and settled fairly close to me. I visited them quite regularly. However, I've often wondered the reason. I must have had some love for them somewhere. After all, they were my parents. I do know that consciously I felt a combination of pity and revulsion.

When I'd look at them—feeble, aging, unhappy, arguing, needy, and still drinking—I'd get that hopeless, helpless sensation in the pit of my stomach.

Driving home after a visit I'd think to myself:

How could you do that to me?
How could you allow others to hurt me?
What were you thinking?
What type of people were you?
Did you expect me never to remember?

Maybe they truly expected me never to remember. Or maybe they expected that I would get addicted to the adrenal rush occasioned during ritual activities and keep my mouth shut even if I did recall.

Regardless, I never brought up the abuse with them. I was terrified that if they had any clue about what I was remembering they might tell members from the ritual group. There would be *hell to pay* for telling anyone about the abuse. It was the old family mantra:

Our secret. Our secret.
Don't tell. Don't tell.

I had already set some boundaries, limiting the amount of time I spent with my parents. My father was unwell and my mother was unable to drive due to failing eyesight. So because of that, I often took her grocery shopping. One particular day she turned to me out of the blue and asked, "Did your father ever sexually abuse you?"

I was stunned but answered truthfully, "Yep."

My mother got a startled look on her face but said nothing more. At that point we got out of the car and went into the store for groceries.

I think my mother was fishing and my answer let her know that I remembered incidents from childhood. Even her question was a type of validation for me: backward and indirect validation, true, but nevertheless validation from a mother who never talked about anything. Obviously my parents' agenda would be to prevent further disclosures to keep them and their friends safe.

True to the patterns of silence in our house, my mother never mentioned the topic again. Of course, neither did I.

After that incident, however, I became even more hypervigilant, fearing that my mother would return home and discuss with my father what I had said. If word got out, I feared there would be repercussions either from them or from other ritual members.

There were repercussions.

I do not know what she and my father discussed. I do know that things changed suddenly and dramatically.

Suddenly my mother's brother and family, with whom I'd been fairly close, broke off all contact with me. Some of my mother's friends, members of clubs my parents had joined, showed up at my office. They grilled me about my life and wanted reasons for my taking a sabbatical from spending time with my parents. After all, they insisted, I was an only child and had obligations to my parents, and on and on went the discussion.

I told my parents' friends that I was fulfilling my obligations as an only child, and I was. I said absolutely nothing about any sexual and ritual abuse, but I also made it clear that there are always two sides to every story. My story was between me and my parents, and I would not be discussing it with them.

Eventually they left.

When the doors closed and I was once again alone in my office, my entire body shook violently. My teeth clattered. I feared that my life was now completely in danger.

For weeks, even months, my hypervigilance was at high peak. Walking on the sidewalk, I would hear the squeal of tires and leap to safety, fearing I would be clipped by the car mirror or even hit.

I talked with my therapist about what had happened, and she recommended that I have no contact with my parents or their close friends. Period. Her recommendation triggered even more anxiety because I struggled with the admonition to *honor your parents*. It had kept me hooked in a sense, pushed me to spend more time with them than was good for me.

The toxic environment just kept the cycle going and kept me from moving forward in my recovery. It was like I had one foot nailed to the floor and was spinning and spinning like a frantic top.

My therapist explained that honoring my parents, especially when they had abused me in childhood, did not require me to spend time with them. I could honor them by becoming the most functional person I could become. I could honor them by recovering from my past and getting healthy. I could honor them by stopping the cycle of dysfunction and becoming the type of healthy individual they had been unable to achieve.

When I finally got this definition, I was both relieved and ecstatic and made huge strides in my recovery. In fact, I was even more motivated to heal and grow. I finally realized, too, that my whole life had been about *them* and their needs, never about me.

After that, I continued to look out for my parents' welfare through hired people. I communicated with the caregivers and not with my parents directly. The decrease in stress was unbelievable. Eventually, when my parents were placed in a retirement center, the move reduced my stress even more. Now they had easy access to professional care 24/7.

Bart and Cookie Baker were very unhappy retirement-center residents, however. Most unhappy and disagreeable retirement-center residents!

The administrator called me one day and asked that I come to the center for a meeting. In fear and trepidation I agreed. There were a couple of problems. For one thing, my father had just discovered that my mother had withdrawn a couple thousand dollars from their joint bank account.

"I sent the money to our granddaughter," she said.

The fat was in the fire. There was no granddaughter. I was their only child and I had no children! That precipitated a huge argument. My mother recalled the city to which she had mailed the money order, but we had no relatives living there. (We were never able to track or retrieve the money.)

For another thing, both my mother and father were complaining about being in there, and adamant about wanting to move back home and/or getting back power of attorney, (which I'd had for more than a decade). The remainder of the meeting was a brutal marathon. For two hours my parents demanded changes. My father was especially angry. Finally the administrator and I concluded there was no point in continuing the discussion.

We left the room and the administrator walked me to the elevator, my father right behind us in his wheelchair. As the elevator door closed, we could still hear his loud, angry voice.

As the elevator descended, there was an awkward silence. I looked at the administrator and decided to address the *elephant* in the elevator.

"Here I am in my early fifties," I said, "and I continue to be absolutely terrified of my father."

There was a very pregnant pause. Finally this tall, stately, professional administrator turned to me. Patting my shoulder lightly, she said, "Your father scares *me*, too."

She was serious, and I felt so affirmed. Wow!

It took me a very long time, years and years, to uncover memories of the abuse. Perhaps this was because it seemed inconceivable that my very own parents, the two adults in the whole wide world whose role it was to nurture and affirm me, to keep me safe from danger and abuse, would do the opposite.

Fortunately, my therapists had refused to buy the scenario I had handed them: *"I had a great family, a wonderful childhood, and good experiences. My parents really loved me."*

Fortunate for me!

> *When one door of happiness closes, another opens: but often we look so long at the closed door that we do not see the one which has been opened for us.*
>
> —Helen Keller

I have always appreciated the fact that my therapists never once offered anything in terms of enhancing my recall or making suggestions. They would say, "Tell me some of your childhood memories."

Initially, my voice whispered out through my drawings. Gradually, little by little, I felt safe enough to find my voice audibly; felt safe enough to start talking out loud. I had to. It had become a matter of life or death.

They just asked—and asked, and asked again, saying, "Tell me some of your childhood memories."

So there was no question of my therapists implanting thoughts into my mind or suggesting abuse where there was none. It was how I answered that question that triggered other memories.

The memories all came from my brain and my body, much of it from my body first. As I'd feel pain in different parts of my anatomy, acknowledge the pain, and be willing to recall, my brain would remember.

Looking back at that now, I am even more in awe of how the body knows. And how the body longs to

> *Our lives begin to end the day we become silent about things that matter.*
>
> —Martin Luther King Jr.

speak if we are open to hearing what it has to say.

Secrets layered upon secrets.

Memories piled upon memories.

Decades of silence.

Decades of silent screams.

My getting into the really heavy-duty memory recall began, interestingly enough, with looking at my dad's drinking patterns and my disappointment in him at some of my softball games (when he'd show up drunk). With my remembering came more recall about how time would go by, weeks on end, when he would never talk to me, never say even one word.

Then it moved on to my mother's role in the family—then her role in orchestrating the rituals. I suddenly remembered how sometimes she put me in the hospital for several days at a stretch. I think these were times when they were planning a ritual gathering. I wasn't sick, so she must have wanted me out of the way temporarily.

Back then, with a doctor and nurse as regular members of the ritual group, admitting me to the hospital and keeping me in the hospital would have been relatively easy.

During the recovery process I also remember feeling like something was missing. Where was that jolt of energy I needed? I had gotten adrenalin to keep me going through sports, but when my physical activity was limited because of my deteriorating health, there now was a sense of dis-ease and a lack of energy.

I know there were times when I took something personally or jumped to conclusions or even overreacted. A subconscious trigger from my brain and body would pour out adrenalin, cortisol, norepinephrine, or would release some other internal chemical that would help me feel alive.

Certainly my brain and body had lost its ability to respond to stressors in a healthy manner. I could neither fight nor flee. Rather, I tended to activate conserve-withdraw, the stress reaction form that leads to immobility. Under stress I would simply freeze like a block of ice, as it were, and be unable to think or to take any constructive action, much like my responses had been during ritual activities.

> *I know that it's easier to look at death than it is to look at pain, because while death is irrevocable, and the grief will lessen in time, pain is too often merely relentless and irreversible.*
>
> —Robert Goolrick

I also exhibited all the symptoms associated with Prolonged Adaptive Stress Syndrome or PASS. No surprise there. No surprise, either, that as with many other survivors I needed help in even identifying some of the symptoms.

When one has lived in a state of discouragement for decades, believing that this is what adulthood means and feels like, it can be difficult to identify discouragement as depression. One by one I am chipping away at the symptoms.

I'm learning the importance of living a balanced life, that I need to take good care of myself and that this is my job: get enough sleep, choose healthy nutritious foods, drink plenty of water, make certain my brain and body receive good micronutrition, connect with nature and my support system, hone my spirituality, and give back to the world.

I am now healthy enough to do that. What a concept. My superego (the brain function piece that enables me to care for myself as I wish healthy functional parents could have cared for me) is operational. In a sense I am reparenting myself. And I'm doing a good job!

> It is important for survivors to remember that it is a mistake to act on these suicidal feelings. There is hope for change today.
>
> —Margaret Smith (pseudonym)

Gratefully, I neither have nor struggle with suicidal feelings as I once did and as is so common among people abused in rituals.

The physical and emotional pain is so intense that the individual may want to numb the pain by hurting his/her body so endorphins, adrenalin, dopamine or other brain chemicals will be released—or stop the pain altogether by committing suicide.

In their book *Facing Shame: Families in Recovery* authors Merle A. Fossum and Marilyn J. Mason wrote:

> *All humans at some time experience injustice, assault, disqualification, invasion and betrayal. No person is completely shielded. We need not trace our family trees very far back or study for long what life was like for our forebears to uncover humanity's abusiveness. The inherited scars of our multigenerational families exist in our family systems as we know them today. The abuse of the past often exists as the shame of today, and the shame is perpetuated through our patterns of interaction.*

I'm still in recovery. I'll always be in recovery. I'm a happy and grateful recovering survivor.

That's okay.

It is what it is.

Every week, sometimes every day, I recognize situations that would have completely immobilized me in the past but which now result in just a little blip on the landscape of my life. I'm grateful for the awareness and the progress.

Frequently, physical illnesses are the body's response to permanent disregard of its vital functions. One of our most vital functions is an ability to listen to the true story of our own lives. There is often a conflict between the things we feel—the things our bodies register—and the things we think we ought to feel so as to comply with moral norms and standards we have internalized at a very early age. When these prevent us from admitting our true feelings, we pay for this compromise with various forms of physical illness.

—Alice Miller
The Body Never Lies

I'm on my way!
Over the rainbow is now!

Chapter Sixteen—
Buds and the Nautilus

*A bridge of silver wings stretches from
the dead ashes of an unforgiving
nightmare to the jeweled vision of a
life started anew.*

—Aberjhani

 I'm nearly finished writing. What an amazing journey—to have found my voice, use it, and finally be heard. It has helped reinforce that I am a survivor, in spades. *I am a survivor!*

The process of writing has helped me view my life from the perspective of a bigger picture. It is allowing me to see the puzzle more completely than ever before. Many, many pieces have fallen into place. That doesn't mean I understand the reasons for everything, but I have been able to connect what happened to me during childhood with some of the consequences to my life in adulthood.

I've always liked quotations, long before I started writing. One of my favorites is attributed to Anaïs Nin, a French-Cuban author. Her words seem representative of my recovery journey:

> *And the day came when the risk to remain tight in a bud was more painful than the risk it took to blossom.*

In a sense I, too, subconsciously had imposed a type of protective loneliness upon myself in order to feel safer. I, too, had experienced a great deal of pain in an attempt to keep the bud intact, that being perceived as the safest course I could travel. I, too, had risked finding my voice, of blossoming into the person I was designed to be.

And over time, slowly, painfully, little bit by little bit, I found that the reward of blossoming clearly outweighed the pain of remaining tight in a bud. As with most things in life, the journey has been up and down. Sometimes incredibly hard. Sometimes so excruciatingly difficult I despaired of recovery and healing. Sometimes surprisingly rewarding and fulfilling. Sometimes so joyfully light I am filled with gratitude to be alive.

My life should never have unfolded as it did. No child's ever should. What happened to me should never have happened. It shouldn't happen to anyone. It does, and it will continue to happen until every individual on this planet embraces the duty to protect children from abuse.

Oh, I realize that every family is dysfunctional. It's part of the human condition. However, there is some dysfunction that's so egregious it needs to be stopped. Period. Innocent children need to be protected from some levels of dysfunction. We can no longer stay silent. I trust that my willingness to finally break my silence will give others encouragement to do the same.

As a child I was not one of the fortunate ones. I was not protected from abuse. Not from emotional abuse, not from sexual abuse, and not from ritual abuse. As an adult I have learned that I can now protect myself.

Furthermore, I am now able to embrace the joy of being a survivor.

It took a very long time, but I have now forgiven my parents for not parenting me lovingly, appropriately. I needed to do that for me. For my health. For my future.

I have forgiven myself, too, for not having been able to take care of me, to protect me. That was a ridiculous expectation anyway. A child cannot parent a child.

I am glad to be alive, moving ever closer to wholeness, enjoying the journey. And I wish that same blessing to anyone who has lived a similar story. I extend to you both my empathy and encouragement.

On several occasions therapists have reminded me that *the truth will set you free ... * and *the only way through is through the pain.* I understand those concepts much more unmistakably now that I'm on the other side of my biggest recovery challenges, if there is such a side. Nevertheless, I love it when I can have something tangible to grasp. That speaks to my kinesthetic sensory preference.

When I came across an object lesson about the chambered nautilus in *The Book of Awakening* by Mark Nepo, I got so excited. (I'm a huge appreciation-fan for object lessons in nature!)

His object lesson about the nautilus not only spoke to me intellectually but also resonated deeply within my very being. I have greatly appreciated its symbolism.

As you probably know, the nautilus is a form of life that lives deep in the sea. As it grows, feeding off the bottom of the ocean, the creature builds an amazing spiral shell. Over time, as the nautilus slowly digests its meals, the food becomes fluid enough to lose most of its weight.

As such, the nautilus always lives in the newest chamber, filling the other chambers with gas to help control its buoyancy.

Recovery is something like that. When I can internalize what I've been through enough to know that I am no longer living there in the past—never to live there again—life seems lighter, more buoyant.

I'm learning to live in the most recent chamber of my heart, so to speak, using the other chambers to stay afloat. I'm understanding and patiently appreciating the fact that only time can put the past in perspective. I'm figuring out that only when the past is behind me am I able to be open and empty enough to sense what is about to happen.

And I now know that only by living in the freshest *chamber* of the heart can I love again and again for the first time.

A nautilus now sits on my shelf. It reminds me that the past is in the past, and I can live and love and express myself fully today, right now. And I can appreciate the moments, allowing myself the opportunity to truly feel.

Bottom line?

Recovery is worth it.

Mark my words.

Recovery is SO WORTH IT!

As a survivor, I have been working through the *Grief Recovery Pyramid.*

GRIEF RECOVERY PYRAMID

There has been so much loss that must be grieved; so much sadness that needs to acknowledged and healed; so little time spent living life to its fullness from a position of joy.

Every day, every week, every month, I recognize progress.

Sometimes the steps are tiny, sometimes larger.

Sometimes the pace is slow, sometimes faster.

My goal is *forward progress* at whatever pace works for my brain and body.

Recovery is about seeing ourselves more clearly and honestly so that we can start being true to who we really are instead of to who our parents wanted us to be. Reacting to the other extreme by rebelling against who they wanted us to be is still living life in reaction to our childhoods. It is still giving power over how we live our life to the past instead of seeing clearly so that we can own our choices today.

—Robert Burney

*I've heard that people stay
in bad situations because a
relationship like that gets
turned up by degrees.*

*It is said that a frog will jump
out of a pot of boiling water.*

*Place him in a pot and turn
it up a little at a time, and
he will stay until he is
boiled to death.*

Us frogs understand this.

—Deb Caletti

Chapter Seventeen—
Free to be Me

You will know the truth—
and the truth will make you free.

—Apostle John

 The last chaper. I'm finally free. And I continue to heal emotionally from a childhood that never should have happened. Not to anyone. Not even once.

Some say I am a courageous woman. I'm starting to let that sink in. And those few who know me well, honor me for my journey. Even more amazing, I am learning to honor myself!

It feels a little strange to realize that this is the last chapter, especially since I was so resistant to writing early on. Who knows? Maybe I'll miss the writing and decide to work on something else. What I do know for sure is that I have a *small village* of friends who continue to encourage and affirm me.

One of them recently wrote these words:

> *You've been through the formative fires of woes and grown from them. Not everyone can do that—bounce back. You are more able to handle life's worries and come out smiling. Hang onto that gift because it brings joy to your heart.*

Growing up I had a sense that I would never live to be older than age 25. I have no idea where that came from, but that is what I believed. And when I didn't die at age 25 I was surprised. Now, however, I am so grateful I did not!

I like the way Dr. Seuss put it in his book *Happy Birthday to You!*

> *Today you are You,*
> *That is truer than true.*
> *There is no one alive*
> *Who is youer than You.*

I am who I am—and "Amelia" is still "Amelia" in many ways. If you knew me once, you would probably recognize me. But in other ways I am very changed. Gone are the stooped postures, bent shoulders, and furtive glances. Gone are many of my physical symptoms (or at least they have lightened considerably), allowing me to once again enjoy walks in nature.

I enjoy my home. And, yes, it is a home!

No longer a house of silence, my *home* is filled with pleasant sounds. Bird calls drift in from the garden. Sounds of the burbling patio water fountain splash gently into the sunshine. Some of *my music* comes out in whistling, which I tend to do unconsciously while I busy myself around the house.

You may even hear the sound of my laughter floating out on the airwaves. I've been told that I possess an innate and dynamite sense of humor. Just that sentence, makes me smile. I think I do too! Outside my childhood home, I was often considered to be a "fun" person. At times I no doubt hid behind my ability to play the *clown*. But now my sense of humor is even displayed at home. I not only tease, but I also feel safe enough to accept being teased. A delight in so many situations.

In much of my past, I needed (or thought I needed) to have every little detail planned so there were no surprises, so that I could feel some sense of safety. Lately it has become much easier to embrace spontaneity. Emotionally, as I continue to grow in that regard, I have raised my emotional intelligence (EQ), since that had been stunted due to the early and very damaging abuse.

Physically, my vision, while not back to its original level, is sufficiently improved to allow me to read—and I do love to read.

There are books everywhere in my home: in the bookcases, on the table, stacked on my desk, and some partially open beside my favorite chair and on my night table.

I collect quotations, too. One of my favorites was sent to me by an old friend who found it on a motivational poster, author unknown:

Life is not about waiting for the storm to pass.
It's about learning to dance in the rain.

Hmmm. Yes, I am learning to dance in the rain, to play in the puddles, and to know that rain comes and goes, clouds drift in and out. While that is true, in between the rain and the clouds, the sky is bright blue.

From time to time, I still exhibit symptoms of hypervigilance, although at a significantly reduced level.

Seated in a community meeting recently, I became very aware of this when another attendee bent down to speak with me, placing her hand on the back of my neck. In the not-so-distant past, a touch like  that would have triggered a huge over-reaction. I would have swatted the person's hand away, leapt up, and rushed from the room.

This time, I did none of these.

Yes, initially, I felt the urge to protect myself. Almost simultaneously, however, I realized that the individual had meant me no harm and had no idea of my personal history. An overreaction would have startled her—and created an unnecessary scene. I was able to connect the physical touch with the urge to protect myself and with the old memories. And I was able to quickly sort through which was which and select the behaviors I wanted to exhibit.

> *Life is not the way it's supposed to be, it's the way it is! The way we cope with it is what makes the difference.*
>
> —Virginia Satir

Note: You may recall my mentioning earlier in the book that I have always been very protective of my head, neck, ears, cheeks, because they were held onto tightly whenever an adult was forcing me to do specific unwanted activities. I still can't wear anything tight around my neck!

This is a great example of the benefit of recovery, of truly understanding that an overreaction in the present often has little if anything to do with the present. In my case (as with most people) it had everything to do with *my* past. Something in the present reminded my brain of the past and (prior to my engaging in the ongoing recovery process) my brain would leap to bring all the unresolved emotion of the past into the present. And wham, bam! It would trigger an overreaction.

My global level of self-esteem is improving, as well.

At times I'm still a bit apprehensive about human touch, but missing is my complete reticence to be touched. I'm learning to give and receive hugs from people with whom I feel safe. And my, that does feel wonderful.

Do recollection, recovery, healing, reparenting, and forgiving offer hope for the future?

Yes, indeed, if the individual is willing to examine his or her family of origin, review and tweak the script that was handed out at birth, put in the work to heal from the damage, and consciously develop more functional behaviors.

> *To forgive is to set a prisoner free—and discover the prisoner is you.*
>
> —Unknown

I not only have survived my past but also have chosen to be cheerful, happy, grateful, and productive on a daily basis. I love my intentionality.

Writing, journaling, and sketching have been part of my recovery work, as have painting, volunteering, and spending time in nature. Some of my friends tease me especially about my love of birds. I adore birds! In some ways they create an extended metaphor for my life.

Newly hatched, baby birds are so fragile and can be injured so easily. In adulthood, however, they are not earth-bound, like most other creatures.

As a child, I was injured and my "wings" were badly damaged. They have healed and I am now flying—sometimes even close to heights that soar.

Yes, to soar!

Will my life forever be impacted by my childhood experiences?

Absolutely.

Any person's life would. After all, a broken bone is never the same after it has been shattered. Amazingly, however, orthopedic surgeons have said that once healed, the bone that was broken is sometimes even stronger than before the injury.

The impact to my brain may have been even more destructive than the physical hurts. As with broken bones, however, survivor after survivor has shown that not only is recovery possible, but also that life after the abuse can be beautiful, fulfilling, and productive. I'm living proof.

I was serious when I told one of my therapists, "If I can become a survivor, anyone can." She agreed.

The bottom line for me?

I uncovered my truth and it set me free. I am no longer in *bondage*.

I found my voice and that empowered me to tell my story.

I chose the hard work of recovery and healing and forgiveness—and moved beyond the house of silence.

> *What you do makes a difference, and you have to decide what kind of difference you want to make.*
>
> —Jane Goodall

As one of my favorite quotations put it: *I shall become myself.*

Indeed. I finally am free to be me.

The truth is, forgiveness does not balance the scales of justice any more than vengeance does. But a failure or inability to forgive creates an inner anger— sometimes observable, but oftentimes unseen—that affects our emotional, spiritual and physical well-being, from broken relationships and cynicism that lead to isolation, to health issues that lead to a shortened life expectancy.

—Dick Tibbits, PhD
Forgive to Live: How Forgiveness Can Save Your Life:

Unconditional
Love—
Good Memories!

Chapter Notes—
Introduction

Admittedly, no parent ever *parents* in a completely competent manner. Unfortunate though that may be, it is what it is. Even when taking on parenting by choice and being committed to hanging in there over the long haul, parents bring to the process their own contributions: some positive, some negative. These include at least Genetics (genes and chromosomes), Epigenetics (cellular memory), personal experiences, innate giftedness, damage and woundedness, unfinished business, addictive behaviors, et cetera.

So the fact that Amelia's parents were unable to provide completely competent parenting did not, in and of itself, account for Amelia's unusual upbringing. But add to a dearth of desirable parenting some very deleterious addictive behaviors, a family atmosphere of silence and anxiety, along with incest and ritualistic gatherings involving fear, loss, abuse, and aberrant sexual activity, a picture quickly emerges of a stressful and terrifying childhood. A childhood that should never have happened.

Not to anyone.

Not even once.

Amelia's story and other similar reported experiences are being validated by authors who are now writing about the costly price of childhood abuse: Steven Farmer, Susan Forward, Robin Karr-Morse, Orit Badouk Epstein, Peter A. Levine, Gabor Maté, Chrystine Oksana, Alison Miller, Randy Noblitt, Pamela Perskin Noblitt, and Margaret Smith, to name just a few.

Evidence of a connection between childhood neglect and abuse and any number of immune disorders and chronic illnesses is accumulating by leaps and bounds as other writers emerge, adding their voices to the body of knowledge. Of particular note are writings by Alice Miller, Christine Caldwell, and Gabor Maté, MD. By pointing out that one's body not only remembers but also doesn't lie, they have focused a clear beam of light and increased understanding on the high price of childhood neglect and abuse, especially related to health.

The Amelia Baker story is the story of one woman, known to the authors. It is an attempt to paint a picture of Amelia's search to find her voice, outline how she began to identify problems and issues she was coping with in adulthood and connect them with childhood experiences. It is an endeavor to chronicle this survivor's frightened and painful efforts at risking the recall and then engaging in the recovery and healing process. Finding her voice and telling her story has encouraged Amelia to remain on the journey of recovery and healing and to continually move forward toward becoming the functional, productive, and happy adult she was undoubtedly designed to be.

In the more global sense, her story points out that abuse still happens and that it requires everyone's voice to prevent future events and to mitigate consequences to those who have already experienced it. The ongoing story is a reminder to survivors of the importance of listening to the body, to the still, small voice inside—that remembers. If Amelia can recover and heal, they can, as well.

The Amelia Baker story also can serve to reinforce the essential value of addressing serious childhood abuse and promoting healing and recovery through a variety of modalities. As with so much else in life, it's different strokes for different folks. Each modality can make its contribution toward healing. These modalities include, but are not limited to Counseling, Psychotherapy, Brain Function information, Physical therapy, Hydrotherapy, Somatherapy, Cranial Sacral therapy, Allopathic medicine, Homeopathic medicine, Drawing, Journaling, Music therapy, Spiritual counseling, and so on.

Amelia worked diligently on this book even when it cost her emotional and physical energy. For example, when the first chapter had been drafted, Amelia could only tolerate listening to it being read aloud if she was standing and moving. It was a visual reinforcement of the reason some therapists encourage their clients to "move around to remember" rather than asking them to sit still in a chair or lie on a couch. When the body is moving, muscle memories seem better able to be released; the tension of remembering better able to be tolerated.

At times as she listened, Amelia would double over with a "kick to the gut," as she put it, or the hairs on her arms or the back of her neck would stand to attention as she recalled some detail that had not yet been discussed. Still she persisted. Over time, some emotional and physical symptoms related to the recall diminished in intensity.

Not everyone is willing to put in the grueling work that genuine recovery requires. It is not for the faint of heart but it is worth it for those who are willing to do the work. Not everyone is willing to follow through in the ongoing process that genuine recovery requires. Amelia is. And in that process, she is freeing herself from the memories that bind and caring for her body in a kind, gentle, and loving way; that wonderful body that chronicled her childhood experiences and remembered. She is moving step-by-step toward improved health and wellbeing. She is healing emotionally from a childhood that never should have happened. Not to anyone. Not even once.

Because Amelia still fears potential retaliation from finding and using her voice and as she sees no purpose in positively fingering her abusers (dead or alive), she has chosen to write under a pseudonym. Some identifying information has been disguised. It is Amelia's decision and hers alone whether or not she will reveal additional details in the future. For now, she feels safe (correct that to *safer)* on her way to healing at all levels. Fortunately, Amelia chose—consciously—to find her voice and move beyond *the house of silence.*

Notes—Chapter 1

Stress, Stressors, and Stress Factors

A stressor can be defined as anything that throws one's body out of homeostatic balance (e.g., injury, illness, subjection to great heat or cold). Anticipation can also serve as a stressor. A child who experiences repetitive types of abuse quickly comes to dread the next episode. Not knowing when the next episode will occur is another stressor. According to Siebert, there is no stress in any situation until the person feels strain and this is different for every brain. The distress felt is not the result of what actually exists objectively, but of how the individual brain perceives what is happening.

According to Dr. Herbert Benson, stress does not cause pain, but it can exacerbate it and make it worse. Much of chronic pain is 'remembered' pain. It's the constant firing of brain cells leading to a memory of pain that lasts, even though the bodily symptoms causing the pain are no longer there. The pain is residing because of the neurological connections in the brain itself.

Daniel Goleman in *The Brain and Emotional Intelligence* uses the term *allostatic load* when referring to a situation when the damaging effects of stress hormones predominate.

Severe stress during the first three or four years of life can actually impair learning centers in the brain, which can damage the person's intellect. When the damaging effects of stress hormones predominate, they can create imbalances in the immune and nervous systems, can harm the hippocampus, impair memory, increase insulin resistance, degrade the myelin sheath, and increase one's risk for diabetes, heart disease, and artery blockages.

Goleman expanded on this in his book *Primal Leadership*. No surprise, distress (negative stressors) erodes mental abilities and makes people less emotionally intelligent. People who are upset have trouble reading emotions accurately in other people, decreasing the most basic skill needed for empathy. As a result, their social skills are impaired.

No surprise, the brain is the first body system to recognize a stressor. It reacts with split-second timing and can stimulate the stress response for up to 72 hours after a traumatic event (real or imagined), making the learning of effective stress-management strategies imperative.

Everyone can benefit from learning effective stress management techniques. This may be especially critical for female brains. Studies by NIMH (National Institutes of Mental Health) grantee Rita Valentino, PhD, have shown that females seem twice as vulnerable as males to many stress-related disorders such as depression and PTSD or Posttraumatic Stress Disorder.

The impact of stressors on learning, memory, and recall is addressed by Hafen in *Mind/Body Health*. Brain cells can be destroyed by stress, especially in the hippocampus, (involved with learning, memory and search-engine functions). The hippocampus may be the brain organ most sensitive to stress.

Studies have found evidence that severe stress can alter brain cells, brain structure, and brain function. Physical and/or mental stress produce neuropeptides that trigger the release of cortisol. High levels of cortisol, especially as seen with chronic stress, can actually destroy brain cells.

Put it all together and memory problems, along with the development of some mental diseases (including depression), may result. Increased levels of cortisol from chronic stressors have been associated with abdominal fat, as well. Consequently, it should not be surprising to discover that survivors sometimes possess incomplete recall. While some details may be burned into the brain, others seem more nebulous or tenuous.

This should not be taken as evidence that the survivors did not experience the abuse. Rather, that the abuse was so stressful that memory and recall functions have been impaired. Trauma alters brain chemistry. Period. This, in turn, results in changed perceptions of reality. When a child is abused or tortured, the child's body releases substances such as adrenaline and endorphins in response to the stress. These substances alter the brain's biochemistry and may even cause hallucinations.

Part of the extremely deleterious effects of ongoing sexual and ritual abuse is due to the phenomenon of *kindling*, a term coined by NIMH researcher Robert Post. The brain appears to develop an increased susceptibility and sensitivity to the next stress episode. What defines stress for each individual is a combination of personal disposition and personal history.

According to the father of stress management, Dr. Hans Selye, an individual experiences excessive stress when the demands made upon him or her far exceed the person's ability or capacity to fulfill them. When this happens, the typical human response to a stressor becomes crippled, damaged, and even deformed. Once that occurs, the stress response can be set off by any number of triggers.

The triggers may include:

- Physical trauma (injury or infection) and/or Emotional trauma (actual or imagined)

- Spiritual trauma (an inability to experience a sense of awe or intense pleasure)

- Psychological trauma (developing erroneous patterns of thinking such as believing that extreme stress is good for one's character development or that the individual did something to warrant the abuse)

- Physiological trauma (living an imbalanced lifestyle, becoming involved in serious addictive behaviors, failing to take good care of oneself).

Being exposed to high levels of acute and chronic stress during childhood can result in a form of conditioning that seriously impacts the person in adulthood. Such individuals often exhibit an impaired ability to engage in vital fight-flight behavior.

In one sense, acute and chronic stress that develops in response to undesirable childhood experiences is not the fundamental problem. Rather it is the environmentally conditioned learned helplessness and hopelessness that blocks the normal response of fight or flight to a stressor. The person can activate neither fight nor flight, the result of which is another type of internal stress. The individual may go into the Conserve-Withdraw stress reaction form. (Think of it as a form of hibernation or freezing.) The brain and body experience a sense of helplessness (if not hopelessness) as if nothing that could be done (if something could be done) would make any difference whatsoever, which can lead to the development of a victim mindset.

When a dreadful loss occurs, the Conserve-Withdraw stress reaction form is helpful in the short term in that it gives the brain and body time to recover. It was undoubtedly never intended for ongoing use, week after month after year. Used inappropriately, it too, can create its own level of stress.

In time, the individual no longer consciously experiences stress from being unable to get his or her needs met or from being expected always to meet the needs of others. The brain and the body are experiencing stress, definitely.

The body systems designed to alert one to danger, however, have been disarmed. Eventually this can contribute to a sense of profound sadness.

Dr. Hans Selye, who borrowed the word *stress* from the field of engineering and applied it to human beings, conceived of stress as a biological process. He perceived stress it to involve a wide-ranging set of events in the human body that occurred irrespective of cause or of the individual's conscious awareness.

Think of stress as consisting of internal physiological alterations that may or may not be visible and that occur when the individual perceives a threat to his or her well-being, if not actual existence. That, of course, means different strokes for different folks. What one brain and body perceives as negative stress may not be perceived as such by a different brain and body.

Studies continue to expand the research around stress and stressors, along with the short- and long-term impact. Three factors have been identified that universally lead to stress. All three have been found to be present in the lives of individuals with serious chronic illness. The three factors are sometimes referred to as the Three L's of Stress:

- Living in a state of uncertainty
- Lack of information
- Loss of any perceived control.

Fight-flight is the stress reaction form that has been most studied.

Work by Shelley E. Taylor, PhD, and others have shown that under sudden stress females may initially exhibit the *fight-flight* stress reaction form. But they soon fall back to a different stress reaction form that the researchers labeled *tend-befriend*.

The more hopeless and helpless the brain perceives the situation to be, the more likely the female is to move into tend-befriend. When using tend-befriend, females try harder, try to do it again and get it right this time. Unmanaged, tend-befriend can lead the female to tolerate the intolerable, resulting in any number of stress-related symptoms and the potential for serious injury or even death, especially when physical abuse is involved.

> *The Hippocampi, tiny brain organs located in the limbic system, are believed to be the most sensitive region of the brain to stress. Prolonged stress can kill cells in the hippocampi as well as in other areas of the brain.*
>
> —Renate Nummela Caine
> Geoffrey Caine.

Women are twice as vulnerable as men to many stress-related disorders. Until recently, an understanding of a possible reason has eluded science. A team of researchers led by Rita Valentino, PhD, of The Children's Hospital of Philadelphia and Debra Bangasser, PhD, Assistant Professor of Psychology at Temple University and a member of the Neuroscience Program used antibodies and an electron microscope to see how the CRF receptor responds in male versus female rats—both unstressed and after exposure to a stressful swim. The researchers reported on their discovery online in the journal *Molecular Psychiatry*. In response to a stressor, Corticotropin Releasing Factor (CRF), both a neurotransmitter and a hormone, binds to receptors on cells in the locus ceruleus, an alarm center deep in the brainstem.

In stress studies involving the female rat, all brain CRF receptors remained exposed on the cell surface, taking the full hit. This increased CRF binding heightens the female brain's stress reactivity. Lack of receptor internalization in the female brain could translate into impaired ability to cope with high levels of CRF, as occurs in depression and PTSD.

On other hand, stress studies of the male rat brain showed that some of the CRF receptors were pulled into the cell. This adaptation, unique to the male brain, toned-down the neuron's stress sensitivity and the load of CRF it absorbed and suggested that the male brain may exhibit less stress reactivity (as compared to the female brain).

Even in the absence of any stress, the researchers found the female stress signaling system to be more sensitive from the start. CRF receptors had stronger connections, or coupling, with relay proteins inside the cell than those of male rats. So it took lower levels of CRF to activate neurons in the unstressed females compared to males. CRF levels that had no effect in males, turned on cells in female rats.

Dr. Allender points out in his book *The Wounded Heart* that sexual abuse sabotages the soul, mocks the enjoyment of relationship, and pours contempt on the thrill of passion. According to Allender, the betrayal involves more than relational sabotage. It is also intensely personal and physical.

Allender writes:

> *Sexual abuse occurs in a context of emptiness, confusion, and loneliness, a context that sets up the victim for a baffling interplay of betrayal, ambivalence, and powerlessness as the adult moves the victim from one stage of abuse to the next.*

Stressors are believed to interact with the brain in a two-part equation: 20 percent of the negative impact is due to the stressor and 80 percent is due to one's own perception. The concept may go back at least to Epictetus, a 2nd Century Greek Philosopher, who taught that it's not so much what happens to you that matters as what you *think* about what happens to you. While you may not be able to do much about the 20 percent (except avoid the stressor when possible), you can do something (if not everything) about the 80 percent. You can adjust the perceived weight or importance you give to the stressor along with your mindset of helplessness and hopelessness.

For example:

- Can you reframe what happened by looking at it a different way or viewing it from a more neutral perspective?

- Are you able to evaluate how much it will matter twelve months in the future? If a lot, give it some thought. If not, let it go.

- Can you identify a humorous aspect and choose to laugh about it?

Dr. Shelley E. Taylor recommended identifying what she has referred to as one's "gold medal moment," a time when something wonderful happened to the individual. Whenever you recognize a stressor or perceive a negative interpretation of an event, recall your own gold medal moment. Thinking about that can help you move into the 80 percent and take charge of your perceptions around the event.

Prolonged Adaptive Stress Syndrome

Survivors of sexual and ritual abuse often exhibit some symptoms of PASS, Prolonged Adaptive Stress Syndrome. Eight commonly observed symptoms may be present in varying degrees in individuals who develop PASS after years of perceiving life was not working for them, and/or from years of living in an environment that was terrifying and/or energy-exhausting:

1. Fatigue
2. Hypervigilance
3. Immune system suppression
4. Reduced frontal lobe function

5. Altered neurochemistry
6. Memory challenges
7. Discouragement or depression
8. Self-esteem issues

Stressors are thought to interact with the brain in a predictable ratio: 20% of the adverse effects being due to the stressors and 80% due to the person's perception of the stressors and the level of helplessness/hopelessness. Adverse effects observed in survivors with PASS may exceed the typical 20%. Such stressors involve not only external and environmental triggers, but internal triggers, as well, including the rate at which the brain itself must work and the amount of energy that must be expended by the individual experiencing the abuse in order to accomplish required tasks or even to survive.

A common side-effect often observed in survivors recovering from symptoms of PASS can be the development of serious addictive behaviors. Over time, the stressors that survivors deal with contribute to an increased risk for self-medicating (altering one's own brain chemistry through the use of addictive substances or through using a variety of addictive behaviors).

Unfortunately, self-medicating through addictive substances or behaviors eventually produces its own stressors—which can contribute to even more pain and suffering and derail the recovery process. If this happens, the survivor then has to deal with not only the recovery from the abuse but also with recovery from the addictive behaviors. The value of effective counselors cannot be overestimated.

Notes—Chapter 2

Child Mistreatment

Child mistreatment or abuse can be defined in many ways. In 2008, in an effort to provide definitions for child maltreatment, Dr. Rebecca T. Leeb and associates published an article on the Centers for Disease Control and Prevention website: *Child Maltreatment Surveillance: Uniform Definitions for Public Health and Recommended Data Elements.*

When children are born, what they need most from their parents is love, by which I mean attention, affection, care, protection, kindness, and the willingness to communicate. If these needs are gratified, the bodies of those children will retain the good memory of such caring affection, and later, as adults, they will be able to pass on the same kind of love to their children. But if this is not the case, the children will be left with a lifelong yearning for the fulfillment of their initial (and vital) needs. In later life, this yearning will be directed at other people.

—Alice Miller
The Body Never Lies

Perpetrators of unlawful violence fall roughly into one of two types: impulsive or premeditated. Interestingly, the US Department of Health and Human Services reported that for each year between 2000 and 2005, female parents acting alone were most likely to be the perpetrators of child abuse.

In 2010, the United States Department of Public Health released statistics outlining the race and ethnicity of all reported instances of child abuse.

Those statistics were:

- White - 44.8%
- African American - 21.9%
- Hispanic - 21.4%

Four major categories of child mistreatment / abuse include these:

- Neglect
- Physical Abuse
- Psychological / Emotional Abuse
- Sexual Abuse

The degree to which the child is impacted by mistreatment / abuse and the severity of symptoms exhibited likely has some correlation with the child's own genetic inheritance, epigenetics (cellular memory), number and duration of mistreatment experiences, and the age(s) at which the abuse took place, to name just a few.

The ramifications to every aspect of his or her life cannot be measured.

The consequences can be glimpsed in exhibited behaviors and/or when the individual is willing to share recollections but likely can never fully be perceived by outsiders. They see only the tip of the iceberg. Children may frequently be the victims of all types of ritual abuse, largely because of their vulnerability and lack of power. Long-term negative outcomes have been associated with child mistreatment / abuse, which may include these:

- Self-blame
- A sense of guilt
- Nightmares, Insomnia
- Flashbacks
- Self-esteem issues
- Boundary problems
- Sexual dysfunction(s)
- Dissociative Identity Disorder (DID)
- Borderline Personality Disorder (BPD)
- Posttraumatic Stress Disorders (PTSD)
- Prolonged Adaptive Stress Syndrome (PASS)
- Sadness, Depression
- Suicidal ideation
- Chronic pain
- Somatic complaints
- Low Emotional Intelligence
- Auto-immune disorders
- A tendency to self-injury
- Disrupted attachment development
- Relationship problems
- Learned helplessness
- A sense of hopelessness
- Development of a victim mindset
- Hypervigilance

The child is often acquainted with his/her offender(s). Almost a third of offenders are believed related to the child either biologically or as in an extended family member, often through marriage.

The offenders, of course, have a vested interest in keeping their actions secret and there are many ways in which to accomplish this.

And, once abuse has occurred, it can take an entire lifetime for the offended individual to connect mental, emotional, physical, sexual, and spiritual problems in adulthood with what happened in the past. Some never do.

Perhaps even more frightening, the negative outcomes may be quite similar regardless of the type of abuse, either experienced personally or witnessed vicariously. How can a child not remember for a time? That can be accomplished with a variety of techniques.

• Being in an environment that creates a sense of perceived terror

• Watching something die or even appearing to die and then being told that unless you do exactly as instructed you will be next

• Experiencing anxiety, fear, and pain to the point that the brain downshifts or dissociates, especially in a child whose brain is not yet developed, downshifts or dissociates

For some individuals, the *forgetting* may last a lifetime.

Notes—Chapter 3

The Emotion of Anger

Anger is considered a core emotion. *Core* because it is one of the emotions that can be seen by scan on the face of a fetus during pregnancy, along with joy, fear, and sadness—depending on what is going on in the mother's body at the time. Considered a protective emotion (along with fear and sadness), anger signals to the individual that his/her boundaries have been invaded, are being invaded, or look as if they may be invaded.

As such, being able to recognize the emotion of anger quickly, perceive the information it is designed to convey, and use the energy created to take appropriate action, is a key strategy for exhibiting high levels of emotional intelligence as well as for successful everyday living.

As a protective emotion, anger can be extremely valuable, even life preserving, when used appropriately. If harbored and hung onto inappropriately, anger can be murderous.

Unfortunately, children who are abused may develop a slush fund of unaddressed, misunderstood (if not outright denied and repressed), unresolved anger. This slush fund can surface at a moment's notice and be exhibited in over-reactions.

The exhibited behaviors may differ in males and females, however, based on how their culture reinforces anger, based on gender. This can be confusing not only for survivors but also for individuals working with them. In many families, any expression of anger on the part of wives or children is not permitted, while it's perfectly acceptable for the father and older male children to express "righteous indignation" in any number of situations.

Not only is it acceptable sometimes for males to verbalize anger openly, expressing it in their behaviors is often tolerated and excused. They may kick the cat, exhibit speed with a motorcycle or vehicle, blame someone else for their anger or for somehow triggering it, get drunk, have an affair, get in a fight, gamble away the family paycheck, and so on.

Conversely, it generally has been considered unladylike for females to become angry, much less express it in behaviors. When they do experience anger, they are expected to talk it out (hopefully calmly) but certainly not act it out. Of course, these are unrealistic expectations, especially in view of statistics indicating that females are responsible for a good portion of child abuse—at least some of which may be based on their own slush fund of unresolved anger.

The Emotions Staircase shows the placement of anger: at the top of two other protective emotions (fear, and sadness), and just below joy. All things being equal, the most appropriate position for the brain to reside would be on the step of joy.

The human brain appears hardwired to live in a state of joy. There appear to be no negative consequences to brain and body when the emotion of joy is maintained over time. On the contrary, there are negative consequences when anger, fear, and sadness are maintained over time.

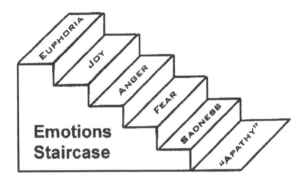

Most people move up to euphoria once in a while to experience that extra little bit of intense joy. They also move down to anger, fear, or sadness when something in the environment warrants the brain doing so.

When the brain becomes overwhelmed with unresolved protective emotions, it can get stuck at apathy. Apathy (not a separate emotion in and of itself) represents an overwhelm of unmanaged emotions to the point that the brain becomes almost immobile in terms of managing any emotion or feeling effectively. When in a state of apathy, individuals may experience a sense of lassitude in which there is little, if any, motivation and/or energy. While individuals may think about suicide when in a state of apathy, they rarely attempt it.

They don't have enough energy! But let things actually start to improve in their lives, and watch out. Let them begin climbing back up the staircase toward joy—and, as they gain some energy, they may attempt suicide. A study entitled "Epigenetic regulation of the glucocorticoid receptor in human brain associates with childhood abuse" reported that childhood abuse (defined in this study as "sexual contact, severe physical abuse and/or severe neglect") leads to epigenetic modifications of glucocorticoid receptor expression, which play a role in hypothalamic-pituitary-adrenal (HPA) activity.

Maternal care influences hypothalamic-pituitary-adrenal (HPA) function in the rat through epigenetic programming of glucocorticoid receptor expression. According to author and researcher P. O. McGowan and colleagues, these findings translate previous results from rat to humans and suggest a common effect of parental care on the epigenetic regulation of hippocampal glucocorticoid receptor expression. In humans, childhood abuse alters HPA stress responses and increases the risk of suicide.

Unfortunately, in many cases of mistreatment, much of childhood was spent circling around in anger, fear, shame, and sadness. This probably accounts for much of the negative thinking patterns that victims develop, patterns that they must work diligently to alter in order to move into a survivor mindset and live life at joy. Anger impacts the body in the same way whether or not the brain perceives that the anger was justified. Adrenalin rises and the nervous system is thrown into a state of alarm.

According to studies by Doc Childre, one five-minute episode of recalling an angry feeling resulted in a short-term rise in immune globulin A (IgA), followed quickly by severe depletion. Six (6) hours were required to restore normal IgA production, with the immune system suppressed for nearly a day.

One single five-minute period of recalled an episode of anger could depress the immune system for almost an entire day. Imagine what a really angry outburst could do! No wonder that survivors who are working diligently on recovery and healing (which typically involve dealing with repressed anger) often experience frequent bouts of illness and are susceptible to colds and flu.

Studies on the brain's adaptation to chronic fear and anger—especially when experienced early in life—have shown potential long term effects. Resulting changes in hormone levels due to ongoing stressors may become permanent in the individual's lifetime.

Borderline Personality Disorder

A larger body of knowledge is emerging related to Borderline Personality Disorder or BPD. Estimates are that BPD affects about six percent of adults, males as often as females. This disorder is characterized by problematic ways of consistently thinking, feeling, and interacting and is associated with an unstable self-image, feelings, behaviors, and relationships.

Perhaps the most distinguishing characteristic is a tendency to see things in black and white. People with BPD tend to live in a world of extremes. This tendency is believed to be closely related to early social interactions and their own self-image.

Like other mental disorders, BPD is understood to be the result of a combination of biological vulnerabilities, ways of thinking, and social stressors. Sufferers are more likely than others to have learning problems. They often come from environments where divorce, neglect, sexual abuse, substance abuse, or death occurred.

Many believe that child abuse or neglect is the main cause of BPD. In childhood, the individual may have experienced a lack of attachment or felt abandoned in some way because they were *bad*. In adulthood, their often frantic efforts to avoid real or imagined perceptions of being abandoned by others because they are *bad* may include impulsive actions such as self-mutilating or suicidal behaviors.

> *Scars are not injuries... A scar is a healing. After injury—a scar is what makes you whole.*
>
> —China Miéville

These individuals can experience intense abandonment fears and inappropriate anger, even when faced with realistic separation or unavoidable changes in plans. For instance, the individual can become very angry with another person who is a few minutes late or who must cancel a lunch date on short notice.

A perception of being abandoned by others may hark back to experiences during early childhood.

Although not considered psychotic, individuals with BPD sometimes feel they can never get enough love and affection to make them feel happy and secure. This not only places a burden on relatives and friends but also prompts others to walk on eggshells to avoid doing or saying something that will upset the individual.

BPD is often identifiable by early adulthood, although an unstable pattern of interacting with others typically has persisted for years. The pattern is present in a variety of settings (e.g., work, home, recreation) and may be accompanied by rapid fluctuations of emotions and feelings. Typically, these individuals are very aware of and highly sensitive to things happening in their environment. At the same time they are often anxious and irritable, suspicious and distrustful, which may relate to early childhood experiences.

Considered to be one of the most common personality disorders, BPD can be difficult to diagnosis because of the varied symptoms that may be exhibited.

Symptoms may include intense fear of abandonment, unpredictable mood swings, emotional intensity, impulsivity, obsessive ruminating, paranoid distortions and self-destructive behavior.

Repression, dissociating emotions from awareness and relegating them to the unconscious realms, disorganizes and confuses our physiological defenses so that in some people these defenses go awry, becoming the destroyers of health rather than its protectors.

—Gabor Maté, MD

Notes—Chapter 4

Ritual Abuse

The term *ritual abuse* has been defined in many different ways.

Following are two examples.

- Psychological, sexual, spiritual, and/or physical assault on an unwilling human victim, committed by one or more persons whose primary motive is to fulfill a prescribed ritual in order to achieve a specific goal or satisfy the perceived needs of their deity.

- A cult-based ritualism in which the abusive activities have a spiritual or social goal for the perpetrators; a pseudo ritualism in which the goal was sexual gratification and the rituals were used to frighten or intimidate victims.

The debate about ritual abuse has raged for years in articles, papers, books, interviews, and discussions.

It has surfaced in the home, the office, in print, in public, and in private. In the majority of cases, the modus operandi has probably been to minimize, if not totally discount, stories that survivors tell about the type and extent of the ritual abuse experienced.

- After all, where are the bodies?
- Where are the instruments of torture?
- Where is the actual, irrefutable evidence?
- Where are the police reports?
- Where is evidence in hospital medical records?
- How could you take the word of a child when his or her parents were upstanding pillars in the community?

This has been the pattern for generation after generation after generation. And because of the skepticism, survivors are universally not offered the type of help that could lead toward healing; not provided with strategies to assist them in detoxifying from the consequences of their experiences.

If diagnosed with Dissociative Identity Disorder, Borderline Personality Disorder, or Posttraumatic Stress Disorder, survivors' symptoms and behaviors typically remain unconnected with any deleterious experiences that might have occurred in childhood (real or imagined). This course of action is undoubtedly in the best interests of any adults involved in perpetuating such abuse for their own dysfunctional rewards. It allows them freedom to continue with their rituals, because who would believe a child reporting such egregious abuse?

Eventually, some authors risked estimates in writing that perhaps ten percent of the allegations of ritual abuse did occur at some level. Several qualified that the abuse may not have actually happened to the child, rather the child might have observed something and misunderstood what was happening or to whom it was happening. Because, again, what adult would perpetrate such egregious abuse on an innocent child?

Soon other studies began to report that it didn't matter whether or not the child had experienced the abuse personally or observed abuse happening to another person. Witnessed vicarious abuse was deemed just as lethal, just as damaging, as abuse personally experienced.

Jean Pierre Barral, author of *Understanding the Messages of Your Body: How to Interpret Physical and Emotional Signals to Achieve Optimal Health,* has said that "the tissues never lie." Indeed, the body *knows*, and this retained knowledge can have a powerfully negative impact on the child's life throughout adulthood in every way imaginable. Even in the absence of explicit memory, implicit memory of the abuse, the terror and sense of helplessness and hopelessness, remain.

According to Siegel, implicit memory involves brain portions that do not require conscious processing either during encoding or retrieval. Somatosensory (bodily) memory and Epigenetics (cellular memory) are likely forms of implicit memory.

A book entitled *Ritual Abuse and Mind Control: The Manipulation of Attachment Needs* is scratching the surface of desperately needed change. Edited by Epstein and Schwartz, it is landmark in both its detail and ability to place ritual abuse in the larger picture of dysfunctional behaviors and their profound and deleterious consequences. The book's editors and chapter-authors have provided a unifying psychological explanation of effects and consequences that result from the bizarre assaults of perpetrators on innocent children.

The book contains solid descriptions of ritual abuse and mind control. The information about abuse and its treatment stands to offer validation and hope not only to many survivors whose stories were never believed or were significantly discounted, but also to many therapists and counselors who were themselves discounted and marginalized as they purported to believe their patients' stories.

In the wake of work by John Bowlby, the legendary twentieth century psychoanalyst of child development, there are compelling explanations of how ritual abuse manipulates the attachment needs of young children; how deliberate, persistent, grotesque, and agonizing perversions against a child can create a psyche almost unrecognizable as human. These afflicted and discredited survivors are the very clients whom the therapist-authors ventured to study and write about, even at high personal and professional risk, speaking clearly about potential dire consequences from the manipulation of attachment needs.

Dr. Ellen Lacter authored the chapter on *Torture-Based Mind Control*. Some readers have said that Dr. Lacter's careful description of psychological mechanisms, such as unconscious implicit memory for trauma and fear conditioning, may be among the best written to date on this topic.

The descriptions of abuse and torture that have been inflicted on tiny children may be difficult for some to even read. Fortunately, Dr. Lacter and others move on to explain the mechanism and tragedy of deliberately interrupting the attachment process and how survivors can be assisted in the recovery and healing processes.

For those who question whether or not ritual abuse really exists and wonder whether it truly can interfere with the attachment process, and for those who may be skeptical about the consequences in adulthood of the attachment process being disrupted in childhood—*Ritual Abuse and Mind Control* may be a requisite read. It may also help survivors and their close support-system members experience validation and hope in a way never before offered.

Ritual abuse tends to take place during structured events in which group members take on assigned roles and typically wear some type of robe or costume. According to some survivors, ritual abuse is designed to betray love, to make the children so hopeless and despairing that it will forever after seem impossible to trust or love again.

Ritual abuse is also designed to make children feel responsible for things about which they had no choice or may not even have done.

Some ritual groups have even set up mock injuries and deaths, designed to look as believable as real killings. Others reportedly have set up scenes where a child is forced to witness a violent act or even commit one. The group members then round on the child, saying that it's the child's fault for whatever happened because he or she is bad (or disobedient, or non-compliant).

Those actions reinforce the eroding sense of self-worth that can cling to the child for decades.

Ritualistic child abuse is the most hideous of all child abuse. The basic objective is premeditated to systematically and methodically torture and terrorize children until they are forced to dissociate. The torture is not a consequence of the loss of temper, but the execution of well-planned, well-thought out rituals often performed by close relatives. The only escape for the children is to dissociate. They will develop a new personality to enable them to endure various forms of abuse. When the episode is over, the core personality is again in control and the individual is not conscious of what happened. Dissociation also serves the purposes of the occult because the children have no day-to-day memory of the atrocities. They go through adolescence and early adulthood with no active memory of what is taking place. Oftentimes they continue in rituals through their teens and early twenties, unaware of their involvement.

—Presiding Bishop Glenn L. Pace
March 2010 statement posted on the internet

Michael Salter, author of *Organized Sexual Abuse,* points out in his book that most perpetrators of organized abuse are men. Their most intensive and sadistic abuses are visited upon girls and women. This has gone largely unnoticed, as have the patterns of gendered inequity that characterize the families and institutional settings in which organized abuse takes place.

Organized abuse survivors share a number of challenges in common with other survivors of abuse and trauma, including health and justice systems that have been slow to recognize and respond to violence against children and women.

Notes—Chapter 5

Family Scripts

Think of a "script" as rules about life and guidelines for living it. It can be spoken or unspoken, written or unwritten. It can involve generalizations or specificity, sometimes to the nth degree of minutia. It contains the spoken and unspoken rules and expectations for your family system, some of which likely are encoded in your cellular memory. Sometimes expectations may begin even before your birth. When these scripts touch on areas of sexuality, religion, or politics, they can be especially powerful.

As Desmond Tutu pointed out so succinctly, "You don't choose your family." Nevertheless, at birth they handed you a script. Your script comes from your parents and forebears, often at least as far back as three or four generations. A problem with the script you've been handed is that every brain is unique, and your brain may not have the same innate giftedness as that of your parents or grandparents.

When this mismatch occurs, parts of your handed-down script may not work for you. In addition, the more dysfunctional the family system (and all family systems have some dysfunction) and the more types of abuse that are present in the environment, the more skewed the script may be. In fact, the script may be absolutely horrible—in and of itself—for a specific child's brain.

Be very clear that on this planet you usually give up something to get something. That's one of the reasons it's so critically important to become aware of and identify the scripts that impact you. You may automatically incorporate those scripts (partially or in total) into your own life, which may be helpful or unhelpful.

Making the script you were handed *your own* can help you avoid blindly following another's script and bring to conscious awareness a sense of what you are giving up and what you are getting by following that script. As usual, what you don't know you don't know has a huge impact on your life. Unless you identify the script you were handed, you often have little or no awareness of its impact on your life and exhibited behaviors.

Some have suggested that healthy, functional maturity involves asking yourself hard questions about your own script and about expectations that you follow the script that was handed to you.

Ask: What does following this script give me? Will I have to give up who I am innately in order to follow this script?

Children tend to absorb and mimic the attitudes and behaviors of their parents and care providers. What if the family script passed down to you was dysfunctional? The outcome depends on many factors, including your own willingness to look at the family script you received, the script you are living out, and the script you are passing on. Without awareness and vigilance, you may pass on some very undesirable expectations to the next generation.

Warren Bennis said this: "To be authentic is literally to . . . discover your own native energies and desires, and then to find your own way of acting on them."

This defines the script you are *living out*.

No surprise that Mark Twain, at age 70, described authenticity in a different way: "You can't reach old age by another man's road. My habits protect my life, but they would assassinate you."

That defines the script you are *passing on*.

Picture a group of actors pouring over scripts: reading, getting feedback, dissecting, rewriting, practicing, doing almost anything within reason to give the performance of a lifetime.

You are the primary actor in your own life. You were handed a script. Evaluate and tweak it as needed. You may need to discard some "scenes" and write new ones.

Your mission—should you choose to accept it—is to identify the script you were handed at birth. Make it your own if for no other reason than someone else's script could discourage, depress, or even try to destroy you. In many cases, doing this process is key to successful living.

Hypervigilance

In his book *Waking the Tiger* Dr. Levine wrote that hypervigilance is one way in which people try to manage the excess energy resulting from an unsuccessful defense against an original threat. Hypervigilance is a strategy that channels some of the energy generated by the defensive attempt into muscles of the head, neck, and eyes. It becomes a protective, and at times an obsessive, proactive search for danger.

When combined with the internal arousal that is still present, rational brains can become irrational and begin to search for and identify external sources of danger. The individuals are continually on edge.

They stand ready to initiate a defensive response (whether or not one is required), but their brains are unable to execute appropriate actions coherently.

Both children and adults can begin to develop habits of extreme intense alertness. As a result of this constant watchfulness, they may exhibit a slightly furtive, open-eyed appearance. Eventually, every change, even in internal states, may be interpreted as a threat. There may be a growing pattern of seeing danger where none really exists. This can result in the development of diminished capacities to experience curiosity, pleasure, or joy in life and may deteriorate into unfounded paranoia.

Awareness is as different from hypervigilance as night is from day. Living in a state of hyperalertness can train the nervous system to stay turned "on" in a state of emergency readiness. When living in this state, both brain and body rhythms may be unsettled and disturbed. For example, the individual may experience disturbed sleep or an inability to fall asleep, or fail to relax and unwind even when he or she feels safe enough to do so.

Hypervigilance can lead to immobility. The individual experiences arousal and automatically feels helpless. As this becomes a learned pattern of behavior, the individual may have a hard time behaving in any way except in hopelessness and helplessness. The sense of helplessness may also become associated with the Conserve-Withdraw reaction to extreme stress, when the brain and body want to hibernate until the danger is past. This can contribute to the immobility that is often observed.

The problem is that the danger never passes, in a sense. Either it continues in actuality or it continues virtually in memory, as the person falls victim to his or her own thoughts, beliefs, internal mental pictures, and personal self-image.

Notes—Chapter 6

Family-of-Origin Work

Family-of-origin work can be described as the deliberate, conscious process of getting to know who you are against the backdrop of nature and nurture. In simplest terms it means identifying and recovering from your past, so you can move forward successfully in the present. Although the term may be relatively new, the work itself represents quite an ancient concept, reaching back at least to Socrates and Plato, both of whom advocated the importance of knowing oneself and deemed the unexamined life not worth living. Your early experiences have a major influence on how you perceive yourself and others, as well as the way in which you learned to cope.

It always comes back to the same necessity; go deep enough and there is a bedrock of truth, however hard.

—May Sarton

Typically your family of origin refers to the first social group you belonged to, which is usually your biological, adoptive, or foster family. The members of your family of origin and our relationships with them (along with your extended family, including ancestors) profoundly influences who you have become. For good or bad, they provide the relational environment—culture, ethnicity, class, and a whole host of social relationships—from which you learn who you are.

What you absorb in your family of origin influences your beliefs, attitudes, expectations, perceptions, behaviors—the way you think. From them you learn how to communicate, manage your emotions and feelings, and get your needs met in healthy ways—or not.

Largely responsible for ingraining beliefs and attitudes, perceptions and values, and setting your sense of self and self-worth, your family of origin provides a base-line for your ability to give and receive love, teaching you how to dream and think, and how to become the person you were intended to be.

Family-of-origin work is not a separate therapeutic method with specific rules and yards of rhetoric. It is a concept, a means for investigating your roots, with the specific purpose of better understanding yourself, your own ways of thinking, your inherited perceptions and beliefs and triggers for your behaviors. Its focus is on discovery and increased awareness. Yours.

Both simple and complex, this work can be useful and valuable. And sometimes it can be life changing. Indeed, some survivors have been able to discover very helpful information about families and behaviors in their generational line, information that jump-started the ability to identify and address behaviors in the current generation.

Picture a cartoon that shows a car stopped by the side of the highway in front of a giant road map. The driver is looking out the window at a large dot on the map. Beside the dot, printed in large bold letters, are the words: *You are here*. The driver's face is a study in stunned disbelief.

Funny, perhaps, but not very helpful. It is difficult to develop a *map* for the rest of your life if you don't know where you've come from.

Without that knowledge, you may spend much of your life driving in circles, metaphorically. This does not suggest that you are to live in the past any more than you are to live in the future. However, to live effectively in the present, you need to know where you've been and identify where you are heading.

Do you find yourself repeating behavioral patterns, reminiscent of a pet hamster running madly on its exercise wheel, never getting anywhere? While exercise can be beneficial to cardiovascular health for an estimated 90% of the population, experiencing your life as a repeating event—when the event is negative or has negative outcomes—is not enjoyable.

Your present reactions to life (especially a tendency to take things personally, jump to conclusions, or overreact) are usually related to your childhood and the learning that took place back then. Some learning was conscious; much was subconscious. Either way, it has an impact on your adult life.

You can invent a healthier future for yourself—by design—when you can identify and put into context who you are against the backdrop of the things that have happened to you over your lifetime.

Family-of-origin work involves three major areas of exploration:

- Innate giftedness – Who you are innately and the types of tasks and activities that energize or drain you

- Personal history – What has happened to you thus far in life including key events, losses, successes, experiences, and patterns of behavior

- Generational inheritance – Patterns of behavior that have been passed down to you from previous generations.

Metaphorically, this process resembles a set of Russian nesting dolls. Peel away each outer doll and another is revealed. Keep uncovering another doll (another layer) and eventually you can reach the core.

There are many avenues to pursue when getting started. Talking with family members and close family friends is one. Use non-threatening personal chats and make it clear this is not about blame. Individuals are often more than willing to reminisce once they understand the reason for your search.

Make it clear that the reason is to help you better understand where you have come from and learn how to exhibit behaviors that result in positive outcomes. Avoid asking "why" questions. Rather, ask *what* they remember about you and your family members.

If speaking with them in person or by phone is not an option, ask for information through letters or e-mails. Do internet searches and read newspapers from your hometown. Look through old photo albums, revisit childhood homes, schools, churches, and cities. These activities can often jog childhood memories.

While it can be important to identify specific events and incidents, what can be even more helpful is an increased awareness of behavioral patterns, both in your life as well as in your generational history. Think of yourself as a detective, connecting puzzle pieces one by one. Together, bit by bit and piece by piece, they create the big picture.

Identifying who you are innately is a life-long process. Every little bit of information (however tiny) adds to your store of knowledge. Every additional puzzle piece adds to the collage. It's amazing how the pieces begin to fit together and how what you learn can assist you in moving steadily toward owning, honoring, valuing, and utilizing your innate giftedness.

Notes—Chapter 7

Attachment

Whether or not a child attaches to and bonds with parents or caregivers impacts self-esteem. The term "attachment behavior" refers to efforts by a child to connect physically, psychologically, and emotionally with primary adults. The biology of attachment points to the crucial period of the first two years when negative patterns are rooted in structural and neurochemical changes. During the first year of life, infants begin to increasingly differentiate their primary parents and caregivers from others.

If no attachment bond forms, all caregivers become equal, and none are considered special. Studies have shown that infants who form secure patterns of attachment readily seek comfort when they are distressed and are calmed more quickly and completely by their attachment figures. Problems can result when the infant either fails to form attachment bonds or when the attachment is fractured through attachment-related trauma.

Identifying what happened in childhood is not about blame. Most people did the best they could at the time with what they knew. Identifying what happened in childhood is about connecting those events with behaviors in adulthood.

It also includes taking responsibility for developing healthier behaviors as would be beneficial.

Four major types of trauma that can interfere with attachment bonds or with attachment processes are described in the book *Adult Attachment – Theory, Research, and Clinical Implications,* edited by Dr. Rholes and Dr. Simpson:

- Attachment disruptions that involve unanticipated and prolonged separation from one or more primary attachment figures

- Physical and sexual abuse at the hands of attachment figures

- Loss of an attachment figure through death

- Attachment injuries including wounds arising from abandonment by an attachment figure in a situation of urgent need.

The abuse creates a unique attachment-related trauma in that the attachment figure (the child's expected haven of safety) now becomes a source of danger. When the trauma becomes repeated and ongoing, the child now has an unending source of stress. In the case of physical and sexual abuse, when the perpetrator is also an attachment figure, this child faces an inescapable dilemma for which there is no solution.

We can feel compassion for our parents. We can feel sad for them. We can empathize with them. But if you pity your parents, then you have been abused by them.

—John Friel and Linda Friel
Adult Children

Some have pointed to Hitler's childhood as an example of this unresolvable dilemma. Reportedly, Hitler's father was an extremely harsh and violent man. Verbal abuse was common in the household, as were whippings. After experiencing beating after beating, little Adolf evidently decided that he would become hardened against pain and suffering. He would never again cry, no matter how hard his father beat him.

Adolf Hitler likely carried the pain of the blows and the anger of its undeserved injustice with him into adulthood. The weight of those hurts and grudges likely played a part in the horror of the Holocaust. Had Hitler been able to heal from his abusive childhood and move beyond the abusive failures of his parents, this would still not have excused his father's behaviors nor his mother's failure to intervene in any way. Had his childhood been less dysfunctional, life for Adolf in adulthood—and life for the world—might have been very different.

Survivors from attachment-related trauma may be more likely to experience emotions and feelings that include frustration, anger, resentment, self-blame, and hopelessness. Some may also be at higher risk for depression.

Unless and until survivors can be helped to heal and recover, they may be at risk for developing symptoms that may include:

- Re-experiencing the trauma(s) in the form of intrusive thoughts or bad dreams

- Becoming emotionally numb in an effort to avoid reminders of the trauma(s)

- Exhibiting irritability, exaggerated startle responses, and hypervigilance in an effort to protect themselves from danger

- Failing to attach even to the self, developing self-esteem issues as a result.

This can result in the self-esteem issues (e.g., too high or too low), the lack of balanced and appropriate self-care, and sometimes a perpetuation of the abuse to the next generation. This is because one's parents and grandparents (and maybe their parents and grandparents) are believed to live on in a person through cellular memories housed on protein strands in the cell nucleus; through visual, auditory, and kinesthetic images that become imprinted on the brain and nervous systems.

Sometimes generational voices can be heard as one's own internal self-talk. Sometimes those voices are allowed to govern one's life much like a posthypnotic suggestion. And when the adult experiences an event that contains any element to remind the brain of the original abusive experience, a flashback can occur.

The imprinted scene will be triggered along with all the visual, auditory, and kinesthetic fragments connected with it. The unfinished business from the past becomes the baggage carried into all current relationships.

According to psychoanalyst Selma Fraiberg, parents tend to bring to the rearing of their children the unresolved issues of the parents' own childhoods. Finishing up their unfinished business may be one of the best gifts parents can give to their offspring.

Finishing up your own unfinished business involves reparenting yourself, taking care of yourself in the way you would have wanted your parents to take care of you had they been capable of doing so. It involves building an optimum level of balanced self-esteem.

Notes—Chapter 8

Downshifting Phenomenon

Downshifting is a natural brain phenomenon. It happens automatically, usually when the brain experiences anxiety, fear, or feels unsafe. Compare it to the way in which an automatic transmission functions. Imagine you are driving in the mountains. The road becomes steep and winding, rain begins to fall, and traffic builds up.

Your vehicle's automatic transmission downshifts into a lower gear, to second or even first—in order to *get through.* If driving conditions become so severe that your vehicle can't get through even in first gear, the engine is likely to stall. Now, picture the reverse situation. The road levels out, the rain stops, and traffic disperses. You expect that your vehicle will now upshift. If it fails to upshift, your vehicle can be a hazard on the highway (e.g., traveling too slowly), requiring additional time and fuel to reach your destination. If the engine overheats and fails, you will need a tow.

The natural brain phenomenon of downshifting appears to fit with what is now known about the triune nature of the human brain: three functional layers. Metaphorically, they resemble gears in a vehicle with an automatic transmission.

Downshifting results in an automatic shift of attention and energy away from the third layer towards the lower, subconscious brain layers. Think of it as a fast slide down a flight of stairs. It can happen in a nanosecond, outside of conscious awareness.

Human Brain Layers

The third layer, neo-cortex or cerebrum or gray matter, houses conscious thought as well as the so-called executive functions. They include decision making, willpower, morality, ethics, goal-setting, and components of the superego.

The second layer, the limbic system or emotional layer or mammalian layer, contains the hippocampus (the brain's search engine) and other little brain organs such as the amygdala. Emotional impulses arise in the subconscious second layer. Not only is it home to phobias but also provides input into operation of the immune system.

The first or reptilian layer contains components of basic brain functions that keep the heart pumping and the lungs exchanging air. Also a subconscious portion, it houses the three main stress responses:

1. Fight-flight – The individual tends to exhibit aggression or runs away

2. Tend-befriend – The individual tries harder and may return to the same environment to do it again in an attempt to get it right this time

3. Conserve-withdraw – The individual becomes temporarily immobile or goes into a form of mental hibernation until the situation changes or the environment is perceived to be safer.

Any situation that involves trauma or crisis, all forms of fear and anxiety and perceived negative experiences, can trigger downshifting. A negative signal from any part of the brain creates a negative response throughout the emotional system, which is then reflected throughout the entire body and brain.

When downshifting is activated unnecessarily or sustained for a prolonged period, learning and development can be impaired in children—and thinking, learning, and decision-making can become faulty in adults.

This may explain the reason that when survivors are unable to get the quality therapy they need, they may become involved in drug use, addictive behaviors, prostitution, all manner of criminal activities, and homelessness.

> *Any anger or fear shifts energy and attention from the neocortex to the reptilian brain.*
>
> —Joseph Chilton Pearce

According to Dr. Dalip Singh, author of the book *Emotional Intelligence at Work*, stress and threat cause the brain to downshift, which reduces the opportunity for neuron growth and inhibits learning. Downshifting and dissociation may even impact each other.

Fear is a protective emotion designed to signal to the brain and body that the individual is in danger. Fear is terrifying to a child, especially when adults are creating the fear and anxiety and no one is coming to the child's rescue. No one is keeping the child safe and preventing further terror. No wonder the brains of children who grow up living in fear learn to dissociate to keep the terror at bay. No wonder the apprehension, sense of threat, and anxiety can trigger the brain to downshift.

Hart, author of *Human Brain and Human Learning,* wrote that the concept of downshifting appears to fit with what can continually be seen happening in instructional settings in typical educational reward-punishment models and in daily living. Learning failure results when threat shuts down the brain. The neocortex, the third brain layer, functions fully only when one feels secure.

If typical reward-punishment styles of education tend to trigger downshifting in the classroom, imagine what parental and/or ritual abuse can trigger. Because any type of abuse can create a sense of being unsafe in the child's mind, it goes without saying that any form of abuse is likely to trigger downshifting.

Some gender differences related to downshifting and outcomes appear to exist. For example, boys seem to have more difficulty coping with parental fighting or divorce. The effects are more intense and last longer. Boys tend to return to stability and learning readiness more slowly, which can have huge implications for education. Some think that boys may actually be at higher risk for downshifting, using as an example the fact that the suicide success rate in males is three times higher than females up to age twenty-four.

On the other hand, girls seem to have more difficulty coping with death or permanent separation. They appear to be more susceptible to stress-related brain shrinkage from cortisol (e.g., five to seven years of over-exposure to stressors may slow the growth of nerve fibers, kill cells in the hippocampus or shrink it).

Part of the craziness that survivors often report related to abuse likely involves what can happen in the brain under conditions of extreme anxiety. Have you seen driver-training cars that contain two sets of controls, including two steering wheels? The student sits behind one steering wheel, the driver trainer behind the other. The student is driving. However, the driver-trainer can grab the wheel and take over any time danger threatens.

Think of the third conscious brain layer as typically doing the steering. Under extreme or chronic anxiety, however, the first brain layer can take over the other set of controls. The third layer continues steering, assuming it is still in charge. It isn't.

And if the anxiety is severe enough, the second brain layer can grab a portion of control.
In effect, this means that the brain's energy and attention becomes distributed among the three layers, rather than being directed toward one layer at a time.

When brain energy and attention become divided, the brain may think one thing (third layer), feel another (second layer), and act from impulses that differ from thoughts or feelings (first layer).

Downshifting happens automatically. Upshifting is a choice based on implementing learned strategies to help one's brain feel safer. This can include immediately going to a sense of gratitude, or thinking of something about which to chuckle, or being able to make a choice.

Being able to choose, to make a decision about almost anything, helps the brain to feel safer. In some cases, this may be enough to help the brain shift its attention and energy back up to the conscious thought part of the brain.

Notes—Chapter 9

Dissociation

Dissociation is a psychological term to describe the process of distancing oneself from physical and emotional discomfort, primarily used to describe the mind's reaction to trauma.

Think of the phenomenon of dissociation as altering a person's thoughts, feelings, or actions so that, for a time, certain information is disassociated from and not integrated with other information as normally happens. It is a strategy used to escape an intolerable situation by detaching oneself mentally and emotionally.

When children are exposed to extreme pain, their minds desperately try to stop it. Sometimes the mind is successful, sometimes not. When successful, children are able to forget at a conscious level the painful abuse they are experiencing.

However, the chronic over activation of neurochemical responses to threat in the central nervous system, particularly in the earliest years of life, can result in lifelong states of either dissociation or hyperarousal.

The amygdala is the brain's alert system. When the child is subjected to negative or painful associations (e.g., sexual violation by a parent), the amygdala will flood the brain with neurochemicals just at the sound of the parent's footsteps. If stimulated intensely or often enough, this alerting system may not subside.

Initially, such occurrences induce chronically fearful states of hyperarousal or hypervigilance in the child. If the child is too young to run or resist, the child will develop a dissociative or "surrender" response. Both dissociation and hyperarousal involve brainstem-controlled central nervous system activity, which produces an increase in epinephrine and other neurochemicals. But unlike hyperarousal, dissociation results in decreased blood pressure and heart rate.

The process of dissociation manifests along a continuum of severity and produces a range of clinical and behavioral phenomena involving alterations in memory and identity. (Traumatic amnesia is common among ritual abuse survivors.)

In dissociation, there is an increase in dopamine-secreting systems, which work together with opioid systems in the brain to produce a calming effect, lowering pain perception, and altering one's sense of time and space.

While dissociating, often a child cannot think. The younger the child is at the time of experiencing terror, the more likely she or he is to respond to the abuse through dissociation rather than through hyperarousal.

Mandated reporting of child abuse in the United States began in the 1960s. Since then, the number of reports to children's protective services (CPS) and law enforcement agencies has steadily increased.

Because most abuse cases occur during the preschool years, children may be particularly vulnerable to dissociation during those years.

In 1999, a study was published in the *American Journal of Psychiatry* entitled *Memories of Childhood Abuse: Dissociation, Amnesia, and Corroboration.*

Two of the study conclusions stated this:

- Childhood abuse, particularly chronic abuse beginning at early ages, is related to the development of high levels of dissociative symptoms including amnesia for abuse memories

- Psychotherapy usually is not associated with memory recovery and independent corroboration of recovered memories of abuse is often present.

Not all abused children develop a dissociation disorder but abused children tend to do so more often than nonabused children. Dissociation reflects disruptions in the integration of memories, perception, and identity into a coherent sense of self. In extreme cases, the process of dissociation gives rise to a set of psychiatric syndromes known as Dissociative Identity Disorder (DID).

Although true prevalence is unknown, DID has been shown to be more common than previously thought. Increasingly, it is being understood as a complex and chronic posttraumatic psychopathology closely related to child abuse. No evidence suggests any biological cause for dissociative identity disorders.

Patients with DID are more likely to have experienced childhood physical abuse and childhood sexual abuse than patients with other psychiatric conditions.

A prospective longitudinal study by researcher Jennifer E. Lansford, PhD, and colleagues (data collected annually from 1987 through 1999) was reported in the Archives of Pediatric & Adolescent Medicine (see Selected Bibliography). "A 12-Year Prospective Study of the Long-term Effects of Early Child Physical Maltreatment on Psychological, Behavioral, and Academic Problems in Adolescence."

The objective of the study was to determine whether physical maltreatment early in life has long-term effects on psychological, behavioral, and academic problems that are independent of other characteristics associated with maltreatment.

The results showed that adolescents maltreated early in life were absent from school more than 1.5 times as many days as nonmaltreated adolescents. They were less likely to anticipate attending college compared with nonmaltreated adolescents, and had levels of aggression, anxiety/depression, dissociation, posttraumatic stress disorder symptoms, social problems, thought problems, and social withdrawal that were on average more than three quarters of a Standard Deviation higher than those of their nonmaltreated counterparts.

The findings held even after controlling for family and child characteristics correlated with maltreatment.

The study concluded that:

- Early physical maltreatment predicts adolescent psychological and behavioral problems, beyond the effects of other factors associated with maltreatment

- Undetected early physical maltreatment in community populations represents a major problem worthy of prevention.

Results of neuroimaging studies have shown that the brains of children raised in violent families resemble the brains of soldiers exposed to combat.

As adults, children who were abused in childhood tend to exhibit high levels of aggression, anxiety, depression, and other behavioral problems, as if they're primed to perceive threat and anticipate pain, adaptations that may be helpful in abusive environments but produce long-term problems with stress and anxiety.

In 1991, the National Child Abuse and Neglect Data System indicated that twenty-four percent of 838,232 reports were for physical abuse and that seven percent of children who were abused were younger than one year of age.

Twenty-seven percent were younger than four years, and twenty-eight percent were ages four to eight years. Early age at onset was also correlated with a higher degree of dissociation.

Exposure to family violence is estimated to impact a significant minority of children.

Notes—Chapter 10

Self-Esteem

According to Dr. Burton White, eminent Harvard physician and child psychiatrist, the first three years of a child's life are all-important in the development of a healthy balanced self-concept.

In fact, one's initial perception of self-worth may be well in place by the age of two. Consequently, it takes concerted effort to change one's level of self-esteem after the age of three.

Every child develops a sense of self-worth that is built and based upon what people say about the child, what is said to the child, and how the child is treated. Like thirsty sponges, children soak up verbal and nonverbal messages rather indiscriminately. Because (at least early on) their frame of reference is inside the family, what children learn about themselves in the context of this environment become universal truths engraved deeply in their minds.

The quality of parenting a child receives is basic to the development of optimum self-esteem as well as bona fide boundaries—both foundational for effective relationships. Nowhere is this more formative than in one's earliest years. Healthy, functional, competent parents provide not only for their child's physical needs but also protect the child from physical harm; provide moral and ethical guidelines (love, attention, and affection), while at the same time protecting the child from emotional harm.

These types of parents understand that nurturing is to the psyche what food is to the body. They are able to help the child feel that he or she is valuable simply because the child exists and is, therefore, worth the parent's time and attention. The child does not have to try to get quality attention from the parent(s).

So called toxic parents not only are unable to provide for their child at this level, they may themselves be so needy that they expect the child to meet their parental needs. They may even expect the child to parent itself. And parents who subject their child to abuse would, by definition, be classified as *toxic*.

Children who grow up experiencing sexual/ritual abuse typically struggle with self-esteem issues. When the parent is unable to adequately nurture and affirm, it can set the child up for a life time of *performing* in an attempt to gain love; to live in adulthood with an overemphasis on *doing* instead of just *being*.

The process of individuation by which you become the person you were intended to become, separate and distinct from others, is a developmental task of childhood. Think of the self as containing three facets of personality:

Core personality

A combination of nature and nurture, your core personality represents who you are innately.

Performing personality

A portion that develops to fulfill your legitimate needs for being noticed, recognized, understood, taken seriously, valued, and respected by others. Think of it as your *performance* on the stage of life.

Protective personality:

A portion that develops as a shield against pain and injury. While the performing personality resorts to relatively benign acts, the protective personality can be more troublesome, exhibiting behaviors that match a belief system that thinks: *I'll get you before you have an opportunity to get me, and then I'll be safe.* When your protective personality is on display, you are usually so busy defending yourself against real or imagined threats that you have little available energy for personal growth or for figuring out who you are, what you need, what you want, and how to go about achieving your goals.

When parents possess optimum levels of self-esteem and the environment is nurturing, children are more likely to develop these three facets of personality in balance. This means they will:

- Develop optimum levels of self-esteem and a realistic sense of personal value (neither less nor more valuable than others)

- Be comfortable with and like who they are

- Know how to get attention or affirmation in ways that result in positive outcomes

- Learn how to protect themselves, how to create and consistently implement bona fide boundaries in ways that neither isolate nor enmesh.

Chapter Notes

Children have basic inalienable rights—to be fed, clothed, sheltered, and protected. But along with these physical rights, they have the right to be nurtured emotionally, to have their feelings respected, and to be treated in ways that allow them to develop a sense of self-worth.

— Susan Forward, PhD
Betrayal of Innocence

When the environment is dysfunctional and caregivers struggle with their own self-esteem problems, the children are more likely to absorb a distorted sense of personal value.

Think of self-esteem as having two general categories, global and specific.

- Global self-esteem involves the degree to which you like, respect, honor, and value yourself as a whole. Compare this to an entire country.

- Specific self-esteem describes the degree to which you like, respect, honor, and value a certain portion of yourself or a specific ability. Compare this to a state or province within a country.

Specific and global self-esteem are both important. An individual who has good levels of specific self-esteem but who lacks global self-esteem (or vice versa) lacks balance in life.

This imbalance can often be seen in children who have been maltreated. No wonder children who grew up experiencing sexual and/or ritual abuse often report serious problems with self-worth.

Notes—Chapter 11

Negative Thinking

Everything begins with a thought—a precursor to words, actions, feelings, and all communication with yourself and others. In order to feel, do, and communicate you must first have a thought, even though you may not be consciously aware of having had the thought.

Many children grow up learning a negative thinking style. It is part and parcel of a dysfunctional family system and no family is truly functional. There are, however, degrees of dysfunction. Children who grew up in a moderately dysfunctional family probably heard nine or ten negative comments or instructions for every positive.

For those who came from a very dysfunctional family, multiply the ratio of negatives to positives by two or three or even four times!

Strong emotional stimuli release hormones and neurotransmitters that help to embed the event in memory. The strength of the memory is related to how important or impactful the experience was to the person at the time. Studies have shown that a person is more likely to recall strong negative emotional states as compared to positive ones. Human beings, especially survivors, need to create positive experiences to encode and recall.

The brain processes information in pictures. It deals easily with positives, a one-step process. Saying what you want to have done is a one-step process. What you say is the picture you want the brain to follow.

Using a negative and saying what you do *not* want involves a two-step process. When you say, "Don't touch the stove," the brain first makes a picture of touching the stove. The word "don't" is designed to direct your brain to create and act on a different picture. It would be more effective to say "Keep your hand away from the stove." That tells the brain what *to do* rather than what not to do, all the while hoping it figures out what to do on its own.

How many times has a child been told, "Don't forget your chores," "Don't forget to practice," "Don't forget your homework," and so on. The brain creates pictures of forgetting and then the child is punished for failure.

The conscious brain layer is capable of processing negatives, given the brain is sufficiently developed to do so. The subconscious layers may be more likely to follow the picture the words created rather than the words themselves. These layers may miss the "don't" and fail to alter the first picture.

Work by Dr. Daniel Wegner has helped to explain this phenomenon. Say, "Don't think about the white bear," and a representation of a white bear goes into your brain's working memory. In fact, the mind cannot seem to rid itself of that thought and will think about the white bear even more.

Willing yourself *not* to do something puts the thing you don't want to do in working memory—the brain constantly thinks about it, which usually increases the behavior. This is especially true if the behavior was one that gave you some comfort or made you feel better.

Therefore, in the recovery process, survivors need to understand the importance of learning to develop a positive style of thinking and speaking and of using their willpower in the way it was intended to function: to help them develop a new behavior or a healthier replacement behavior.

Body energy is closely connected with your thoughts and mental pictures. Positive thoughts and feelings add energy to your system while negative thoughts and feelings deplete your energy. Anxiety and anger are "energy eaters." No wonder children who are experiencing abuse are often fatigued; no wonder survivors tend to experience exhaustion as they work through the recovery process.

A negative mindset, a negative thinking style, can turn into a vicious cycle and drag you down. That's partly because the brain tends to pursue congruity. When in the grip of a strong emotion, the brain tends to trigger recall of past situations that involved a similar emotion in order to promote congruity. The brain wants everything to match.

- Sadness, anger, or fear trigger recall of sad, angry, or fearful memories. Negativity triggers recall of negative memories. The stress response can be extended in both brain and body by dwelling upon the negative aspects of an event

- Positive thoughts trigger recall of positive memories. Positive emotional states create coherence within the human system.

Virtually no energy is wasted when all components of a system are operating in positive congruity. Jon Gordon, author of *Energy Addict: 101 Physical, Mental, and Spiritual Ways to Energize Your Life,* wrote:

> *If you think positively about the day ahead, you increase both your mental and physical energy.*

This is not to suggest embracing a Pollyanna approach to life. Bad things happen, which need to be identified, grieved, and resolved insofar as is possible. Once they are acknowledged and addressed, think positively.

You may not be responsible for every thought that crosses your brain. You are responsible for the thoughts you hang onto and for the actions you take around them.

The power of positive is very strong. That's one reason affirmation is often referred to as the programming language of the brain. Affirmation is the label for a thinking style that emphasizes being grateful and happy and that uses positive words to communicate with yourself and others.

Moving toward thinking more positively can begin by something as simple as becoming mindful of your thoughts, especially passing thoughts. Learn to pay *non-evaluative* attention, realizing that your thoughts are just mental events. They are not synonymous with who you are, not necessarily reflections of reality, and not something you must act upon now or even later.

When you recognize that a thought is negative, you can make some choices.

1. Is this a thought I want to keep harboring and dwell upon?

   Yes or no. If the answer is no, replace the thought with a healthier, more positive replacement thought.

2. Is this a thought I want to take action upon?

   Yes or no. If the answer is no, use willpower to implement a healthier, more positive replacement action.

Suppose you become aware of a thought that says, "I am worthless."

- First, you can change your relationship to that thought and think: *Oops, there goes that unhelpful thought again.*

- Second, you can choose to replace that thought with a healthier replacement thought such as: *I am valuable simply because I exist.*

According to Doc Childre and Howard Martin, authors of *The HeartMath Solution,* your habitual attitudes form neural circuits in your brain. If you choose to maintain a specific attitude (e.g., choose to change your thoughts from negative to positive), the brain can literally rewire itself to facilitate that attitude.

During childhood, abused children live in a state of almost constant anxiety, fear, terror, and negative thinking.

Part of the recovery process involves altering one's habitual thought patterns so the brain can rewire itself to facilitate a more positive thinking style and attitude.

Notes—Chapter 12

Learned Helplessness

Seligman has written extensively on the topic of learned helplessness. The state of learned helplessness (actual or imagined) is a potential trigger for biological stress responses. It can be described as a learned psychological state in which people fail to extricate themselves from stressful situations. Seligman's foundational experiments and theory of learned helplessness began quite by accident, as an extension of his interest in depression.

The researchers noticed that when animals were repeatedly caused discomfort by an adverse stimulus which they could not escape (e.g., mild electric shock), eventually about two-thirds of the tested animals stopped trying to avoid the pain and behaved as if they were utterly helpless to change the situation. Eventually, when opportunities to escape the discomfort were presented, the learned helplessness prevented the animals from taking any action.

The only coping mechanism the animals used was to become stoic. This helped them put up with the discomfort and avoid expending energy getting worked up about the adverse stimulus.

There are several interesting aspects of human helplessness that appear to have no counterpart among animals. One of the most intriguing is vicarious learning. Just as studies have shown that the effects of witnessing abuse can be as damaging as personally experiencing it, people can learn to become helpless through observing another individual encountering uncontrollable events.

Another aspect is that symptoms of learned helplessness (e.g., depressed mood, feelings of worthlessness and low self-esteem, suicidal ideation) can be found and observed in human beings, but not necessarily in animals.

As mentioned, not all of the animals tested developed learned helplessness. The one third that did not managed to find a way out of the unpleasant situation despite their past experience.

A corresponding characteristic in humans has been found to correlate highly with optimism and an explanatory style that tends to view the situation as *other than* personal, pervasive, or permanent.

In humans, learned helplessness may result when the person stops trying because he/she truly believes there is no dependable cause-and-effect relationship between his/her efforts and the outcomes, i.e., nothing can be done to alter the circumstances or situation.

Initially, this may have been because the individuals were physically unable to remove themselves from the actual experience, although they may have extricated themselves psychologically by means of dissociation. Later on, due to their history of learned responses, they may remain in an abusive personal or professional relationship or may stay stuck in a lifestyle that contributes to disease and to *dis-ease* in a myriad of different ways.

An experiment was carried out with people who performed mental tasks in the presence of distracting noise. The individuals who could use a switch to turn off the noise showed improved performance, even though they rarely bothered to use the switch.

Simply being aware of this option was enough to substantially counteract its distracting effect. In studies of animals and humans, the strongest predictor of a depressive response was a perceived lack of control over the aversive stimulus.

According to Eric Jensen, author of *Brain-Based Learning*, learned helplessness is just that: learned. It describes a chronic condition in which the brain has decreased amounts of serotonin, norepinephine, GABA, and dopamine, along with increased levels of cortisol. The good news is that because helplessness is learned, it can be unlearned.

The bad news is that individuals often need help in unlearning patterns of hopelessness and helplessness. Consequently, survivors will likely need to find a therapist or support person that can give feedback regarding their behaviors along with self-talk strategies to help them choose a positive mindset and encouragement to utilize willpower in the recovery process.

The new discipline of psychoneuroimmunology has now matured to the point where there is compelling evidence, advanced by scientists from many fields, that an intimate relationship exists between the brain and the immune system... An individual's emotional makeup, and the response to continued stress, may indeed be causative in the many diseases that medicine treats but whose [origin] is not yet known—diseases such as scleroderma, and the vast majority of rheumatic disorders, the inflammatory bowel disorders, diabetes, multiple sclerosis, and legions of other conditions that are represented in each medical subspecialty...

—Gabor Maté, MD
When the Body Says NO

Quoting Noel B. Hershfield, clinical Professor of Medicine at the University of Calgary

Notes—Chapter 13

Gender Processing Styles

All human brains are designed to problem solve at some level. Studies have provided generalizations about the way this process occurs. It appears to differ somewhat by gender.

For example, the male brain tends to problem solve and reach a conclusion most effectively when it processes information silently and internally. It prefers to state its conclusion only at the end of the processing period.

Female brains typically operate differently. While it takes about the same amount of time to reach a conclusion, the female brain generally tends to problem solve most effectively by talking aloud about the information, verbalizing options and possibilities. In a sense, the female brain comes to conclusions by listening to itself speak aloud. As one woman said, "How do I know what I think 'til I hear myself saying it?"

> *Generalizations are conclusions from studies that typically apply to about 2/3 of the population.*

In addition, the female brain tends to relieve internal stress by talking about things, rehearsing. In these situations, females are not necessarily processing aloud in an effort to reach a solution, but rather to help themselves make sense of things. Many females have been socialized to keep quiet about what they think, or have learned to do so because of experiences involving pain, shame, or fear. When this happens, the information can bang around inside a woman's brain and cause all manner of distress and confusion.

Sometimes the information is repressed from conscious awareness, which still can cause all manner of distress, confusion, immune system suppression, depression, and you name it. Because the symptoms are unconnected to a consciously recalled experience, however, the health-care emphasis on resolving the symptoms may fail to address the underlying stress and distress.

Females tend to verbalize aloud. They tend to problem solve by speaking audibly about options and possibilities. They also tend to vocalize about the list of things they need to do. Males tend to talk mainly inside their heads. They can be with other males for long periods of time using very little audible speech.

—Barbara Pease, Allan Pease
Why Men Don't Listen and
Women Can't Read Maps

Notes—Chapter 14

Brain-Body Connection

It is impossible to separate brain from body. (Dr. Candace Pert referred to them as the bodymind.) Socrates was teaching that perspective thousands of years before the science of PNI or psychoneuroimmunoendocrinology came into being. Current studies are validating Socrates' position.

Just so it is impossible to separate emotions from illness. Dr. Maté, author of *When the Body Says NO – Exploring the Stress-Disease Connection,* points out that individuals typically do not become ill despite their lives but rather because of their lives. The body is a fount of innate wisdom. Much disease could be healed and much prevented if people understood the existing scientific evidence verifying the mind-body connection.

Saying that repression is a major cause of stress and a significant contributor to illness, however, is no agenda for any type of blame, shame, or pointing of fingers. The goal is to identify a relationship between stress and disease as a physiological reality.

When individuals repress their emotions in an attempt to survive, this inhibition may disarm the body's defenses against illness.

For individuals engaged in recovery from abuse who are pursuing the healing process, every bit of information uncovered, every piece of truth surfaced, may be crucial to the desired outcome.

Consider some of the diseases that are being identified as autoimmune, e.g., scleroderma, rheumatoid arthritis, systemic lupus erythematosus, ulcerative colitis, diabetes, multiple sclerosis and now maybe even Alzheimer's disease. Their commonality is the body's own immune system turning against itself and creating havoc. The resulting "internal civil war" may rest upon the negative impact of stress to the immune system, whereby the stress is transmuted into illness.

Dr. Robert Maunder, psychiatric faculty member of the University of Toronto, has affirmed the benefits of attempting to uncover the stressors and their interface with the strong mind-body connection in disease. He says, "Trying to identify and to answer the question of stress is more likely to lead to health than ignoring the question."

According to author Margaret Smith (pseudonym), ritual abuse survivors experience overwhelming pain and trauma-related symptoms as they remember the ritual abuse. They experience violent flashbacks. Their bodies feel the same sensations as at the time of attack. This is the same traumatic memory process experienced by other torture survivors and by war veterans traumatized on the battlefield.

Even though the survivor may have traumatic amnesia, the physical sensations still remain in the body even when there is no conscious mind to describe the sensations. After the actual trauma has stopped, the physical sensations tend to recur in the body as body memories.

According to Alice Miller, *the body never lies.* It remembers exactly what happened. Body memories are the grounding force for all the confusion in the survivor's mind. In fact, it is often from such body memories that survivors can reconnect with the original pain. This, in turn, leads to the emotional and conscious truth of what they experienced.

It can be literally lifesaving to use the information to promote recovery and healing.

Personal Boundaries

Although human beings are born with virtually no boundaries, they have the ability to learn to set healthy limits, a process that ideally begins at an early age. Children absorb information about boundaries from watching their care providers and role models just as they learn almost everything else in infancy. Initially, children are relatively helpless and their boundaries are comingled with those of their care providers. In fact, they only perceive themselves through the mirror of care providers. Whatever they think and feel, the child thinks and feels. There is only "us."

A sense of self begins to emerge at about the age of six months that is integral to the development of personal boundaries. Children who are not permitted to develop appropriate boundaries during childhood—their boundaries are nonexistent or too rigid—tend to have serious boundary problems in adulthood.

When personal boundaries are broken or nonexistent, individuals may become almost instantly empathetically enmeshed with other individuals. This presents problems with identity and with protecting themselves because they don't know where they begin and end, and the other person begins and ends.

When personal boundaries are too tight and rigid, individuals are unable to connect with others empathetically and appropriately. They may experience a sense of isolation, as if walled off from the warmth of human connection by a wire barricade. They cannot seem to let anyone in, at any level, or for any reason.

Sometimes these individuals swing quickly from a position of becoming almost instantly enmeshed with other individuals to the opposite position of living life with rigid, almost impenetrable, boundaries in order to feel safe. Personal boundaries that are inappropriately loose or too tight can result in a type of chronic stress that brings its own problems.

Think of bona fide boundaries as a fence with a working gate. A latch on the inside allows individuals to open the gate, or close and lock it, depending on the circumstances. Individuals can let others in as appropriate, while at the same time protect themselves from situations where others need to remain outside.

The blurring of psychological and physical boundaries in childhood can become a significant source of stress in adulthood. The body's hormonal and immune systems experience ongoing negative effects because people with indistinct or inappropriate personal boundaries live with stress as a permanent part of their daily life. Initially, at least, many of them have no idea of the impact boundary problems create, having learned to exclude any such direct awareness from their consciousness.

And then there are boundary violations. Call them by whatever name you wish, they represent abuse: any inappropriate action or interaction related to one's personal limits; any experience or attitude imposed on an individual (consciously or subconsciously) that interferes with the development of healthy responses or behaviors. The abuse can occur as neglect, trauma, or catastrophe, and may be the result of a one-time incident or an accumulation of experiences distributed over time. Actions and interactions can be abusive without being either continuous or profound. Even desirable behaviors (e.g., pleasing others), taken to extremes, can result in the development of boundary problems.

This can prevent individuals from becoming all they could have become and from achieving all they could have achieved had the boundary violations not occurred.

When the abuse begins long before the child is capable of clear verbal communication, the child may not be able to describe exactly what happened. In addition, prior to age seven or eight, many children have difficulty distinguishing between reality and illusion.

Children from dysfunctional family systems characterized by boundary violations are at higher risk for: developing problems with self-worth, exhibiting obsessive/compulsive behaviors, struggling with addictive behaviors, experiencing relationships difficulties, exhibiting a variety of emotional problems, and failing to establish bona fide boundaries.

- **Overt** boundary violations tend to be easily recognizable behaviors that are obvious and involve a direct assault on the person (e.g., bullying, slapping, or spitting). Someone attacks, criticizes, strikes, screams at, belittles, or judges the child harshly, causing the child to feel devalued, shamed, and even worthless.

- **Hidden** boundary violations are more subtle and more difficult to detect. They are often mislabeled within the culture and may be seen in behaviors that run the gamut from excessive teasing to outright neglect or isolation.

- **Vicarious** boundary violations involve the witnessing of abuse that is inflicted upon others. Witnessed (or vicarious) abuse can result in consequences and problems similar to those that occur when an individual personally experiences the abuse. In terms of damage, there appears to be little difference in whether the abuse is experienced personally or just observed happening to someone else.

Note: Whether a child experiences abuse personally, witnesses it happening to someone else, or watches an illusion created to convince the child that *I did this*, or *It happened to me,* there is little if any difference in outcome. Neurons in the brain (sometimes called mirror neurons) fire when the brain is watching an event just as if the brain were experiencing or participating in the event itself. Since each brain is unique, each will respond to abuse differently and develop different strategies in an attempt to survive. Some children may develop patterns of over-conforming, outright rebellion, addictive behaviors, or depressive thinking that can lead to suicidal ideation.

The human brain was designed to process only so much raw emotion at one time . . . Watching a personal tragedy or a natural disaster on the morning news is a qualitatively different experience from merely reading about the tragedy. The video image is processed primarily with the right hemisphere of the brain; it bypasses language, reason, and logic.... We cannot cope with a sustained assault of elemental emotions like fear, horror, and outrage. If enough horrors are repeatedly depicted with sufficient graphic impact, in a self-protective reflex the brain simply shuts down. Hideous images cease to arouse any emotion except, perhaps, boredom... The pornography of violence is every bit as ugly and brutalizing as sexual pornography—probably more so.

—Richard Restak, MD
The Brain Has a Mind of Its Own

Notes—Chapter 15

Survivor Recovery

According to Margaret Smith (a pseudonym), survivors who grew up experiencing ritual abuse (especially those who grew up in cults), tend to have the most difficult time breaking free. Once a person, a family, is caught in a ritual-abuse cycle, it can be very hard to break the pattern.

This may be due in part because extreme trauma results in a lack of emotion. This lack can then result in the capacity to abuse others with little or no remorse. Some authors believe this indicates just how disconnected and isolated abusers are from their own emotions and feelings.

Results of a study reported in the book *Ritual Abuse* indicated that more than half of the survivors who participated in rituals said that their parents were the abusers. Relationships with family members constitute the primary childhood relationship. The fact that parents can abuse their own children betrays this most primary relationship.

When adults steal a child's right to be cared for safely—emotionally, physically, and sexually—the violating acts are reflective of the abusers' own pain. They are capable of hurting children without apparent remorse because of their own emotional isolation.

The actual ritual experiences themselves can become addicting

> *Nothing solidifies a memory like emotion… Some intense emotions may have the opposite effect: in childhood sex abuse, for example. That powerful trauma is suppressed and can be retrieved only with intensive therapy….*
>
> —Deepak Chopra, MD

due to the rush of brain chemicals released during the activities. For individuals habituated to high levels of internal stress since early childhood, the absence of stressors may initially create unease, a sense of meaninglessness, even boredom.

This is due to individuals becoming addicted to their own stress hormones: adrenaline and cortisol. Until and unless these individuals get into recovery, the consequences triggered by the stressors can feel desirable; while the absence of the stress hormones feel like withdrawal. This can keep them chained to repeating the ritual activities.

Of course, a primary motive of ritual abuse is to make the child feel ashamed and helpless. The more ashamed, helpless, and hopeless the child feels, the easier for the adults to control the child. The easier, as well, for the adults to relieve some of their own internal discomfort by abusing someone who is younger and weaker.

One of the challenges during recovery is that survivors often experience such a sense of hopelessness that they think about death. Some report feeling utterly helpless, like birds trapped in locked cages. When they perceive no escape from their lives of suffering, suicide can appear the quickest and most appealing solution.

Suicidal feelings may also surface through the memory process. As survivors begin to remember the abuse, they experience the same feelings as during the abuse. This is a natural part of the memory process. Without an understanding of the pain, however, the survivor may believe the suffering will last forever.

Part of recovery involves finding qualified therapists who provide a safe environment for the survivor to recall the trauma, work through the emotional and physical pain, view the experiences with adult eyes, separate from the abusive environment (if that is needed), and heal. It comes as no surprise that adult survivors of ritual abuse generally need more precautions to protect themselves than do those who have not been ritually abused.

Recovery also needs to address any ideas and beliefs that were deliberately programmed into the survivor's psyche during the abuse. This is especially critical if the survivors were involved with a cult. Survivors often recall being programmed by cult leaders. This may include specific directions on how to behave outside the cult, to never talk with anyone about the abuse, whom to associate with, and what to believe about themselves and other group or cult members. It may involve imprinting on the child where to go to school, what type of career to select, and whom to marry.

In an effort to keep the children bonded to the group, leaders commonly teach the younger members that they are superior to others. They try to create a sense of "specialness," which is typically the only so-called positive feeling the children are allowed. Survivors have reported all manner of programming strategies. Typically the strategies involve forms of inflicting pain that did not leave marks. These can include:

- Electric shock
- Poking body parts with needles
- Sexual violence
- Other forms of torture, often in association with hypnosis.

Survivors have also reported that a doctor was usually present at indoctrination rituals to advise members doing the torturing what to do and how to do it in order to avoid leaving marks. After the ritual ceremony, the doctor was also available to treat injuries and to coach members on exactly how to explain away the children's injuries in case school officials or law enforcement asked questions. If the physical damage inflicted by the parents on their child created noticeable injuries, the parents were often instructed to keep the child home from school. The excuse provided to the school was that the child had a cold or flu. When the injuries vanished from sight, the child would return to the classroom.

Because of the magnitude of the abuse and the way in which it impacts both mind and body, recovery can be a long process—a very long process indeed. As a ball-park figure, some have estimated that at a minimum it requires a month of solid recovery work for every year of abuse, and that's once the individual has memories of being abused. It's less a destination than a life-long journey of healing.

For people who have been severely traumatized, the violent memories become frozen in time. Later, after the actual danger has ceased, survivors begin to recall the trauma first in their bodies. There may be flashbacks in which mind and body reenact the traumatic experience. For some, there is a sensation, situation, object or phrase—a trigger—that begins the process of conscious memory. The memory and recovery process described by ritual survivors is remarkably similar to that of war veterans and incest survivors.

The bottom line is that recovery is possible; it can and does occur. The individual wanting to recover and heal must be serious about and willing to do the hard work. The journey can be facilitated by working with knowledgeable, skilled, and empathetic health care professionals.

Notes—Chapter 16

Grief Recovery

Loss hurts. There's no way around that. One's emotions and feelings are closely intertwined with both loss and with the grieving process.

The emotion of sadness signals that you have experienced a loss. Learning to quickly and accurately recognize the emotion of sadness is critical in being able to use the energy it generates to help you take appropriate action and move through grief recovery at a pace right for you.

Typically, there is a tremendous amount of loss that survivors need to grieve and release. There can be loss related to inadequate parenting, loss related to a terrifying childhood, loss related to sexual and ritual abuse, loss of a functional and healthy childhood, loss related to illness or injury. Loss layered upon loss. For some, there is the additional burden of feeling guilty for having even survived.

It's the age-old question: *Why me?*

But there's another way to ask that question:

Why not me? Some are learning to ask the question in that style.

There can be a vast difference between the grieving process useful in preparation for one's own death and grief recovery that is effective for survivors. The Kubler-Ross work has been landmark in helping individuals prepare to die with dignity.

The Grief Recovery Pyramid, on the other hand, is designed to help survivors move through grief recovery successfully. Some can even experience some sense of guilt because they lived through the abuse when others did not. They can learn to affirm themselves for surviving!

GRIEF RECOVERY PYRAMID

©Arlene R. Taylor PhD

289

The recovery process is a journey, as unique as each survivor's brain. Some move through the stages of recovery more quickly than others; most move around and back and forth several times. Levine, in his book *Waking the Tiger: Healing Trauma,* argues persuasively that psychological scars of trauma are indeed reversible. The body, a healer, can heal. But only if one listens to the voices of the body, finds its own voice and speaks.

In general, behavioral patterns related to loss and grief recovery are learned. They reflect what people saw role modeled by caregivers, personal experience, cultural conditioning, the instructional script that was handed to them, along with expectations, to name just a few. If your learned patterns are ineffective, you can learn more effective behavioral patterns that can help you recover successfully from loss and free up vital energy. As survivors become empowered to deal more effectively with their own trauma and losses, they become better equipped to offer encouragement and affirmation to others during episodes of loss and grief recovery.

Cellular Memory

Human beings are a combination of nature (genetics) and nurture (epigenetics). Building blocks in the cell nucleus transmit information from generation to generation making you who you are as a distinct individual.

Some of the building blocks involve deoxyribonucleic acid or DNA, a molecule containing genetic instructions (genetics involving genes and chromosomes); some involve strands of regulatory proteins containing information that can impact the DNA (epigenetics involving cellular memory).

Most people are familiar with the concept of genetic inheritance involving genes and chromosomes and the double helix (DNA). Fewer are familiar with the concept of epigenetic inheritance. The science of epigenetics has determined that a variety of environmental influences including nutrition, emotions, and stress, are able to:

- Act upon genes and chromosomes, turning them on or off

- Impact how genes are expressed, without changing any of their actual DNA blueprint

- Imprint and store memories in strands of regulatory proteins in the cell nucleus (of cells that contain a nucleus)—cellular memory is the common term for this form of non-declarative memory.

Cellular memory may influence a person's preferences, choices, and behaviors. Some believe this explains the phenomenon of *past lives.*

Books now have been written documenting cellular memory believed pasted on through organ transplants.

Because donor organs carry cellular memory, transplant recipients may have surprisingly accurate dreams about the donor, especially with heart transplants. Recipients of an organ transplant may also experience definite alteration in food tastes and other preferences post-surgery.

Cellular memories may help to explain how specific behavioral and disease patterns show up frequently in specific generational lines, albeit inconsistently, as well as the behavioral differences often observed not only among siblings but also in children who have been adopted.

Muscle cells contain a nucleus, as do neurons in the brain, heart, G I Tract, spinal cord, and nervous system. (Red blood cells do not.) Thus, a potential for virtually whole-body memory exists. If the individual has a kinesthetic sensory preference, the potential for re-experiencing recalled cellular-memory pain in muscles and joints may be enhanced.

Cellular memory may play a part in the perpetuation of ritual, sexual, or other forms of abuse to succeeding generations. Thus, when parents participate in ritual abuse, this cellular memory may be transmitted to their biological offspring. When a woman is pregnant, she passes along cellular memory that she received from her biological ancestors as well as the cellular memories she herself created. This impacts the developing fetus and its biological offspring, and so on. It is no surprise, therefore, that cellular memories may contribute to the generational continuation of patterns of abuse.

Notes—Chapter 17

Physiology of Forgiveness

Every person has some story involving hurtful events, often perpetrated by a person who mattered in his or her life. Confusion often surrounds the controversial topic of "forgiveness," to say nothing of misunderstandings related to definitions.

There may be as many definitions of "forgiveness" as brains that consider the topic. One definition is simply giving up your right to make another person pay (beyond what the law requires) for his/her actions toward you. Another says forgiveness involves giving up your right to exact retribution from the individual who hurt or wronged you. You:

- Choose to think about something else rather than harbor resentment in working memory

- Refrain from repeatedly bringing up the incident to yourself and/or others and rehearsing all the details

- Move from a victim mindset to that of a survivor mindset.

As Dr. Herbert Benson put it: "There's something called the 'physiology of forgiveness.'® Being unable to forgive other people's faults is harmful to one's health."

To refrain from forgiving increases the likelihood that you may create a virtual enemy outpost inside your head. An enemy outpost requires a great deal of energy to maintain. It also nearly guarantees that the "enemy" is within, and the memory of the hurt is readily available for frequent rehearsing.

Being a victim involves feelings of helplessness and hopelessness, and often a sense of being *special* because the person has been injured. It can be helpful to assist the person in understanding that everyone is injured in some way in the war zone of planet earth. A victim mindset can keep a person stuck—as it burns up norepinephrine (a brain-body substance that helps deal with stress), stops emotional growth, and blocks recovery.

The goal is to move from a victim position into a survivor mindset. Survivorship is the badge of honor. Developing a survivor mindset can assist the injured individual to:

- Recover
- Grow up emotionally
- Heal wounds from the injury
- Role model a survivor mindset
- Help others

Forgiveness can help facilitate this process.

As recently as a few years ago, it would have been difficult to find much information on the physiology of forgiveness. Few people knew that *forgiveness research* even existed. Although the field is relatively new, it has grown exponentially over the past decade with more than 1,200 published studies (up from 58 as recently as 1997).

> *One of the secret causes of stress plaguing millions of people is unforgiveness.*
>
> —Don Colbert, MD

Studies have shown that there is not just a psychology underlying forgiveness but a physiology as well.

An inability or unwillingness to forgive has been linked with a variety of health hazards and negative consequences, which may include:

- Increased stress levels and muscle tension

- Increased blood pressure and heart rate

- Increased levels of adrenaline and cortisol

- Suppressed immune function

- Increased risk for depression, heart disease, stroke, and cancer

- Decreased neurological function and memory

- Impaired relationships at home and at work.

Fortunately, there is a flip side, as with many things in life. On the flip side, studies have revealed the immense power of forgiveness, which may include:

- Healthier relationships

- Greater mental, physical, and spiritual health

- Less anxiety, stress, and hostility

- Lower blood pressure

- Fewer symptoms of depression

- Lower risk of alcohol / substance abuse

- Making room for compassion, kindness, and peace

- Improved overall health and wellbeing.

At least two types of forgiveness pop up in the literature: decisional forgiveness and emotional forgiveness.

1. Decisional forgiveness involves a behavioral intention to resist an unforgiving stance and to respond differently toward a transgressor (in one's thoughts and actions).

2. Emotional forgiveness involves the replacement of negative unforgiving emotions with positive other-oriented emotions. The psychophysiological changes generated have more direct positive consequences for a person's health and well-being.

Forgiveness and forgiving appear to be crucial to healthy living. As the Doctors Arnold and Barry Fox put it: "When you say 'I forgive you,' you're also saying 'I want to be healthy.'"

The act of forgiving allows the body to turn down the manufacture of catabolic chemicals, and instructs the subconscious to banish negative feelings from the mind.

Genuine forgiveness involves giving careful thought to identifying what happened, the life-long consequences, and what needs to be done for recovery and healing. It involves systematically following through with choices and behaviors, including these:

- Identify and label the abuse honestly, specifically, and completely

- Assume responsibility only for your part (if any) in the event

- Discover, accept, and connect the negative consequences of the abuse with problems in your adult life

- Give up continually rehearsing all the gory details to yourself and/or to others

- Develop and implement appropriate personal boundaries

- Deliberately craft an abuse-free lifestyle.

The process of genuine forgiveness may include cooperation with the culture/society/legal system, which may require that the perpetrator be punished for his/her actions. It may mean that contact with a specific individual is infrequent and prescribed. It could mean a cessation of any contact for a period of time. Sometimes that period of time may need to be forever.

Bottom line

Forgiveness has far less to do with other individuals, including perpetrators and offenders, and everything to do with the forgiver. Studies have shown that it is the *forgiver* who benefits the most.

Authors and Resources

Marilyn J. Banford PhD, has an earned doctorate in counselling as well as a B.Ed and a M.A.P.M. She is frequently asked to present workshops and to address audiences on topics that range from grief recovery issues and managing stressors effectively to enhancing one's spirituality.

Banford serves as a teaching consultant at local hospitals and enjoys being in the out-of-doors. She also serves as a preferred provider / consultant for a leading National EFAP Organization (Employee & Family Assistance Program), counseling and helping employees and their families resolve work, health, and life issues that can interfere with productivity and engagement.

Banford primarily offers counseling in areas related to dealing with Anxiety, Anger Management, Depression, Grief Recovery, and Stress Management.

Contact Dr. Banford at: mjb47@shaw.ca

Arlene R. Taylor PhD, an internationally known speaker on brain function, is sometimes referred to as the brain guru. She specializes in simplifying this complex topic—thereby assisting individuals to unleash their potential to thrive. A sought-after speaker, Taylor has spoken to thousands of people at conferences internationally. She presents practical brain function information in practical, entertaining, educational, and empowering ways.

Taylor is founder and president of Realizations Inc, a non-profit corporation that engages in brain function research and provides related educational resources. A member of the *National Speakers Association* and listed with the *Professional Speakers Bureau International*, she has two earned doctorates. Author of more than two dozen books and syllabi, many of her books and DVDs are available on Amazon.com. Synapsez®, her quarterly electronic *Brain Bulletin*, is available at no charge. Sign up at Taylor's website: www.arlenetaylor.org

Articles/Monographs, Brain Aerobic Exercises, Brain References, Questions & Answers, and other website resources are also available at no charge.

Contact Dr. Taylor at: thebrain@arlenetaylor.org

Follow, like, and share Taylor's daily blog
http://arlenetaylor.blogspot.com/

Selected Bibliography

This selected bibliography includes resources that Amelia found and still finds helpful in her recovery journey, along with additional resources and references.

Allender, Dan B., MD, PhD. *The Wounded Heart - Hope for Adult Victims of Childhood Sexual Abuse.* CO:Navpress, 1993.

Bangasser, Debra, PhD, and Rita Valentino, PhD. *Stress Hormone Receptors Are Less Adaptive in the Female Brain.* http://www.nimh.nih.gov/science-news/2010/stress-hormone-receptors-less-adaptive-in-female-brain.shtml?WT.mc_id=twitter&sms_ss=email URL accessed 11/12.

Barral, Jean-Pierre. *Understanding the Messages of Your Body: How to Interpret Physical and Emotional Signals to Achieve Optimal Health.* CA:North Atlantic Books, 2008.

Beattie, Melody. *Codependent No More Workbook.* NY:Hazelden Publishing, 1986.

Beattie, Melody. *Codependent No More: How to Stop Controlling Others and Start Caring for Yourself.* NY:Hazelden Publishing, 1986.

Benson, Herbert, MD, with Marg Stark. *Timeless Healing.* NY:Scribner, 1997.

Benson, Herbert, MD, and Miriam Z. Klipper. *The Relaxation Response.* NY:HarperTorch, 2000.

Blakeslee, Sandra. "Studies Show Talking With Infants Shapes Basis of Ability to Think." http://www.nytimes.com/1997/04/17/us/studies-show-talking-with-infants-shapes-basis-of-ability-to-think.html?pagewanted=all&src=pm URL accessed 11/12.

Borderline Personality Disorder (BPD). URL example accessed 9/12

Borderline Personality Disorder Research Foundation, 340 West 12th Street, New York, NY 10014 http://www.borderlineresearch.org

Bradshaw, John. *Bradshaw on the Family: A Revolutionary Way of Self-Discovery.* FL:Health Communications, Inc., 1988.

Bradshaw, John. *Creating Love – the Next Great Stage of Growth.* NY:Bantam Books, 1992.

Bradshaw, John. *Healing the Shame That Binds You.* FL:Health Communications, Inc., 2005.

Bradshaw, John. *Home Coming; Reclaiming and Championing Your Inner Child.* NY:Bantam Books, 1992.

Branden, Nathaniel. *How to Raise Your Self-Esteem.* NY:Bantam Books, 1998.

Branden, Nathaniel. *The Disowned Self.* NY:Bantam Books, 1984.

Brownmiller, Susan. *Against Our Will: Men, Women and Rape.* NY:Bantam Books, 1993.

Caine, Renate Nummela, and Geoffrey Caine. *Making Connections: Teaching and the Human Brain.* VA: ASCD, 1991.

Caldwell, Christine. *Getting Our Bodies Back.* MA:Shambhala, 1996.

California State Department of Education. *Toward a State of Self-Esteem.* CA:Bureau of Publications.

Carder, Dave, MA, et al. *Secrets of Your Family Tree. Healing for Adult Children of Dysfunction.* IL:Moody Press, 1995.

Carder, Dave, M.A., et al. *Unlocking Your Family Patterns: Finding Freedom from a Hurtful Past.* IL:Moody Publishers, 2011.

Carter, Rita, Ed. *Mapping the Mind.* CA:University of California Press, 1998.

Child Maltreatment. *U.S. Department of Health and Human Services.* URL accessed 10/12. http://www.acf.hhs.gov/programs/cb/pubs/cm10/cm 10.pdf#page=31

Childre, Doc. *Freeze Frame.* CA: Planetary Publications, 1994, 1998.

Childre, Doc, and Lew and Deborah Rozman. *Overcoming Emotional Chaos.* CA:Jodere Group, 2002.

Childre, Doc, and Howard Martin. *The HeartMath Solution.* CA: Harper SF, 1999.

Clance, Pauline Rose. *The Impostor Phenomenon.* NY:Bantam Books, 1985.

Clemes, Harris and Reynold Bean. *Self-Esteem: The Key to Your Child's Well-Being.* NY:Kensington Publishing Corp., 1981.

Cloud, Henry, PhD, and John Townsend, PhD. *Boundaries.* MI:Zondervan, 2004.

Cloud, Henry, PhD, and John Townsend, PhD. *Safe People: How to Find Relationships That Are Good for You and Avoid Those That Aren't.* MI:Zondervan, 1996.

Davis, Laura. *The Courage to Heal Workbook: A Guide for Women and Men Survivors of Child Sexual Abuse.* NY:Harper Perennial, 1990.

Dissociative Identity Disorder. Accessed 11/13.

- http://emedicine.medscape.com/article/916186-overview

- http://www.nami.org/Content/ContentGroups/H elpline1/Dissociative_Identity_Disorder_(forme rly_Multiple_Personality_Disorder).htm

Dweck, Carol S., PhD. *Mindset: How we can learn to fulfill our potential.* NY:Ballentine Books, 2006.

Edwards, Katherine. *A House Divided: The Secret Betrayal – Incest.* MI:Zondervan, 1990.

Epstein, M. Donald, DC. *Healing Myths, Healing Magic: Breaking the Spell of Old Illusions.* CA:Amber-Allen Publishing, *2000.*

Epstein, M. Donald, DC, and Nathaniel Altman. *The 12 Stages of Healing: A Network Approach to Wholeness.* CA:Amber-Allen Publishing, 1994.

Epstein, Orit Badouk (Editor), Joseph Schwartz (Editor), Rachel Wingfield Schwartz, and Ellen Lacter PhD. *Ritual Abuse and Mind Control: The Manipulation of Attachment Needs.* MI:Karnac Books, 2001.

Farmer, Steven. *Adult Children of Abusive Parents. A Healing Program for Those Who Have Been Physically, Sexually, or Emotionally Abused.* CA:Lowell House, 1990.

Fisher, Helen, PhD. *Why We Love: the Nature and Chemistry of Romantic Love.* NY:Henry Holt and Company, 2004.

Forward, Susan. *Emotional Blackmail: When the People in Your Life Use Fear, Obligation, and Guilt to Manipulate You.* NY:William Morrow Paperbacks, 1998.

Forward, Susan, with Craig Buck. *Betrayal of Innocence: Incest and Its Devastation.* NY:Penguin Books, 1988.

Forward, Susan, PhD, with Craig Buck. *Toxic Parents: Overcoming Their Hurtful Legacy & Reclaiming Your Life.* NY:Bantam Books, 2002.

Fossum, Merle A., and Marilyn J. Mason. *Facing Shame: Families in Recovery.* NY:W. W. Norton & Company, 1989.

Fox, Arnold, MD, and Barry Fox, PhD. *Beyond Positive Thinking: Putting Your Thoughts into Action.* VA:The Napoleon Hill Foundation, 2011.

Fox, Arnold, MD, and Barry Fox, PhD. *Wake Up! You're Alive!* Executive Books, 1988.

Fraser, George A. (Editor). *The Dilemma of Ritual Abuse: Cautions and Guides for Therapists.* American Psychiatric Publication, 1997.

Friedman, Edwin H. *Generation to Generation* NY:The Guilford Press, 2011.

Friel, John and Linda Friel. *Adult Children: The Secrets of Dysfunctional Families.* FL:Health Communications, 1990.

Garber, J. and Seligman, M.E.P. (Eds.). *Human Helplessness: Theory and Applications.* NY:Academic Press, 1980.

Gazzaniga, Michael S. *Who's in Charge.* NY:HarperCollins, 2011.

Goleman, Daniel Jay, PhD. *The Brain and Emotional Intelligence: New Insights.* MA:More Than Sound, 2011.

Goleman, Daniel Jay, PhD, with Richard Boyatzis, and Annie Mckee. *Primal Leadership.* MA:Harvard Business School Press, 2002.

Gordon, Jon. *The Energy Bus: 10 Rules to Fuel Your Life, Work, and Team with Positive Energy.* NY:Wiley, 2007.

Gordon, Jon. *Energy Addict: 101 Physical, Mental, and Spiritual Ways to Energize Your Life.* NY:Perigee Trade, 2004.

Hafen, Brent Q., et al. *Mind/Body Health.* MA:Allyn & Bacon, 1996.

Hall, Lindsey and Leigh Cohn. *Self-Esteem: Tools for Recovery.* CA:Gurze Books, 1993.

Hart, Leslie, A. *Human Brain and Human Learning.* NY: Longman Inc., 1983.

Hendricks, Gay. *Learning to Love Yourself.* CreateSpace Independent Publishing Platform, 2011.

Hendricks, Gay. *Learning to Love Yourself Workbook.* NY:Prentice Hall, 1990.

Huber, Cheri, and June Shiver. *There is Nothing Wrong with You: Going Beyond Self-Hate.* IL:Keep It Simple Books, IPG, 2001)

Huber, Cheri, and June Shiver. *How You Do Anything is How You Do Everything.* IL:Keep It Simple Books, IPG, 1988.

Jack, Dana Crowley. *Silencing the Self: Women and Depression.* NY:HarperCollins, Publishers, 1991.

Jensen, Eric P. *Brain-Based Learning: The New Paradigm of Teaching.* NY:Corwin, 2008.

Karr-Morse, Robin and Meredith S. Wiley. *Ghosts from the Nursery –Tracing the Roots of Violence.* NY:The Atlantic Monthly Press, 1998.

Katherine, Anne, MA. *Boundaries Where You End and I Begin: How To Recognize and Set Healthy Boundaries.* NY:Hazelden, 1994.

Kellogg, Terry, with Marvel Harrison. *Broken Toys; Broken Dreams.* MA:BRAT Publishing: Amhurst, 1990.

Ketterman, Grace. *Verbal Abuse: Healing the Hidden Wound.* MI:Servant Publications, 1993.

Langer, Ellen J. *Counterclockwise: Mindful Health and the Power of Possibility.* NY:Ballantine Books, 2009.

Langer, Ellen J. *Mindfulness.* MA:Da Capo Press, 1990.

Lazarus, Richard S., PhD. *Stress and Emotion: A New Synthesis.* NY:Springer, 2006.

Lansford, Jennifer E., PhD, et al. "A 12-year prospective study of the long-term effects of early child physical maltreatment on psychological, behavioral, and academic problems in adolescence." Accessed 11/12. http://www.ncbi.nlm.nih.gov/pmc/articles/PMC275 6659/

LeDoux, Joseph. *Synaptic Self.* NY:Penguin Books, 2002.

Leeb, Rebecca T., PhD, et al. "Child maltreatment surveillance: uniform definitions for public health and recommended data elements." Accessed 11/13. Http://www.cdc.gov/ViolencePrevention/childmaltr eatment/definitions.html

Leman, Kevin, PhD, and Randy Carlson. *Unlocking the Secrets of Your Childhood Memories.* TN:Thomas Nelson Publishers, 1989.

Levine, Peter A. *Waking the Tiger: Healing Trauma.* NY:North Atlantic Books, 1997.

Lombard, Jay, DO., and Christian John Renna, DO. *Balance Your Brain, Balance Your life.* NJ:John Wiley & Sons, Inc., 2004.

McGinnis, Alan Loy. *The Power of Optimism.* NY:Harper & Row, Publishers, Inc., 1990.

McGonigal, Kelly, PhD. *The Willpower Instinct: How Self-Control Works, Why it matters, and What you can do to get more of it.* NY:Penguin Books, Inc., 2012.

McGowan, P. O., et al. "Epigenetic regulation of the glucocorticoid receptor in human brain associates with childhood abuse." http://www.ncbi.nlm.nih.gov/pubmed/19234457 Accessed 3/14.

McWilliams, Peter. *You Can't Afford the Luxury of a Negative Thought.* NC:Mary Books, 1995.

Martin, Grant L. *Counseling for Family Violence and Abuse.* TX:Word Publishing, 1987.

Maté, Gabor, MD. *When the Body Says NO: Exploring the Stress-Disease Connection.* NJ:John Wiley & Sons, Inc., 2003, 2011.

Mayer, Robert. *Through Divided Minds.* NY:Doubleday, 1990.

Mayer, Robert. *Satan's Children: Studies in Multiple Personality.* NY:G.P. Putnam's Sons, 1991.

Middelton-Moz, Jane, and Lorie Dwinell. *After the Tears. Reclaiming the Personal Losses of Childhood.* FL:Health Communications, Inc., 2010.

Miller, Alice. *The Drama of the Gifted Child: The Search for the True Self.* NY:Books, Inc., 2008.

Miller, Alice, and Andrew Jenkins. *The Body Never Lies: The Lingering Effects of Hurtful Parenting.* NY:W. W. Norton & Company (1 Reprint edition), 2006.

Miller, Alison. *Healing the Unimaginable: Treating Ritual Abuse and Mind Control.* London:Karnac Books Ltd, 2011.

Miller, Mary Susan. *No Visible Wounds. Identifying Nonphysical Abuse of Women by Their Men.* NY:Ballentine Books, 1996.

Muller, Robert T. *Trauma and the Avoidant Client: Attachment-Based Strategies for Healing.* NY:W. W. Norton & Company, 2010.

Myers, John E.B., J.D. *The APSAC Handbook on Child Maltreatment.* CA:Sage Publications Inc., 2010.

Nepo, Mark. *The Book of Awakening: Having the Life You Want by Being Present to the Life You Have.* CA:Conari Press Publishing, 2011.

Noblitt, Randy, and Pamela Perskin Noblitt. *Ritual Abuse in the Twenty-First Century.* OR:Robert Reed Publishers, 2008.

Oksana, Chrystine. *Safe Passage to Healing: A Guide for Survivors of Ritual Abuse.* IN:iUniverse Publishing, 2001.

Ornstein, Robert, PhD. *The Roots of the Self.* NY:HarperCollins Publishing, 1995.

Pace, Glenn L, Presiding Bishop. *Satanic Abuse Exposed.* Accessed 11/12. http://www.mormonstruth.org/LDSoccult.html

Pearce, Colby. *A Short Introduction to Attachment and Attachment Disorder.* London:Jessica Kingsley Publishers, 2009.

Pease, Barbara and Allan Pease. *Why Men Don't Have a Clue and Women Always Need More Shoes.* NY:Broadway Books, 2004.

Pease, Barbara, Allan Pease. *Why Men Don't Listen and Women Can't Read Maps.* NY: Broadway Books, 1998.

Pearsall, Paul, PhD. *The Heart's Code.* NY:Broadway Books, 1998.

Pelzer, Dave J. *A Child Called "It" – One Child's Courage to Survive.* FL:Health Communications, Inc., 2000.

Pelzer, Dave J. *A Man Named Dave – A Story of Triumph and Forgiveness.* NY:Plume Publishing, 2000.

Pelzer, Dave J. *The Lost Boy: A Foster Child's Search for the Love of a Family.* FL:Health Communications, Inc., 1997.

Pert, Candace B., PhD. *Molecules of Emotion: The Science Behind Mind-Body Medicine.* NY:Simon & Schuster, 1999.

Pert, Candace B., PhD. *Molecules of Emotion: Why You Feel the Way You Feel.* NY: Scribner, 1997.

Pert, Candace B., PhD. *Your Body Is Your Subconscious Mind* (Audiobook). CO:Sounds True Inc., 2000.

Peterson, C., Maier, S., and Seligman, M.E.P. *Learned Helplessness.* NY:Oxford University Press, 1993.

Poole, Carolyn. "Maximizing learning: a conversation with Renate Nummela Caine." Educational Leadership, Vol 54, No 6, 3/97.

Promise, The. *New Testament Contemporary English Version.* TN:Thomas Nelson Inc, 1995.

Restak, Richard, MD. *The Brain Has a Mind of Its Own.* NY:Three Rivers Press, 1993.

Rholes, W. Steven, PhD, and Jeffry A. Simpson, PhD., Editors. *Adult Attachment –Theory, Research, and Clinical Implications.* NY:The Guilford Press, 2004.

Ritual Abuse URLs. Examples accessed 11/12.

- http://www.amazon.com/gp/reader/088048
  4780/ref=sib_books_pg?p=S02E&keyword
  s=satanic+ritual+abuse+principles+of+treat
  ment&ie=UTF8&qid=1313943088#reader_
  0880484780

- http://blog.lotusopening.com/2010/03/mor
  mon-bishop-glenn-pace-charges-utah.html

- www.religioustolerance.org/ra_intro.htm#d
  ef

- Wikipedia.org/wiki/Satanic_ritual_abuse#D
  efinitions

Ross, Colin A., MD. *Satanic Ritual Abuse –
Principles of Treatment.* Canada:University of
Toronto Press Inc., 1995.

Salter, Michael. *Organized Sexual Abuse.*
*NY:*Routledge, 2012.

Sapolsky, Robert M., PhD. *Why Zebras Don't Get
Ulcers.* NY:W. H. Freeman and Company, 1994.

Schechter, Daniel. S., et al. "Disturbances of
attachment and parental psychopathology in early
childhood." *Infant and Early Childhood Mental
Health Issue. Child and Adolescent Psychiatry
Clinics of North America,* 18(3), 665-687, 2009.
http://www.ncbi.nlm.nih.gov/pmc/articles/PMC269
0512/?tool=pubmed Accessed 11/12.

Seamands, David A. *Healing for Damaged Emotions.* CO:David C. Cook, 1991.

Seligman, Martin E.P., PhD. *Helplessness: On Depression, Development, and Death.* Second edition. NY:W.H. Freeman, 1991.

Shemmings, David, Yvonne Shemmings. *Understanding Disorganized Attachment: Theory and Practice for Working with Children and Adults.* London:Jessica Kingsley Publishers, 2011.

Siebert, Al, PhD. *The Survivor Personality.* NY:A Perigee Book, 1996.

Siegel, Daniel J. *The Developing Mind.* NY: The Guilford Press, 1999.

Singh, Dalip, PhD. *Emotional Intelligence at Work.* NY:Sage, 2000.

Smith, Margaret (pseudonym). *Ritual Abuse: What It Is, Why It Happens, and How to Help.* CA:Harper San Francisco, 1993.

Tanzi, Rudolph E., PhD and Deepak Chopra, M.D. *Super Brain.* NY:Harmony Books, 2012.

Taylor, Arlene R., PhD, and W. Eugene Brewer, EdD. *Your Brain Has a Bent (Not a Dent),* Third Edition. CA:Success Resources International, 2014.

Tibbits, Dick, PhD, with Steve Halliday. *Forgive To Live: How Forgiveness Can Save Your Life.* TN:Integrity Publishers, 2006.

Townsend, John, PhD. *Beyond Boundaries: Learning to Trust Again in Relationships.* MI:Zondervan, 2011.

Townsend, John, PhD. *Hiding from Love.* MI:Zondervan, 1996.

Valentino, Rita, PhD, NIMH grantee. "Women are twice as vulnerable as men to many stress-related disorders, such as depression and PTSD." Accessed 11/13. http://www.nimh.nih.gov/science-news/2010/stress-hormone-receptors-less-adaptive-in-female-brain.shtml?WT.mc_id=twitter&sms_ss=email)

Wegner, Daniel M., PhD. *White Bears and Other Unwanted Thoughts: Suppression, Obsession, and the Psychology of Mental Control.* NY:Gulford Press, 1994.

White, Burton L., MD. *New First Three Years of Life - Completely Revised and Updated.* NY:Touchstone, 1995.

Whitfield, Charles L. MD. *Healing the Child Within: Discovery and Recovery for Adult Children of Dysfunctional Families.* FL:Health Communications, Inc., 1987.

Wright, Veronica. *Boxes of Secrets.* Amazon Digital Services, Inc., 2010.

Selected Bibliography